Safely Onward

The History of the Unitarian Church of All Souls

New York City

Volume 3: 1882-1978

Walter Donald Kring

Contents

Illustrations:

Safely Onward

God be with thee! Gently o'er thee
May his wings of mercy spread;
Be his way made plain before thee,
And his glory round thee shed.
Safely onward, safely onward,
May thy pilgrim feet be led.

Hymn by Theodore Chickering Williams (1889)

The fourth and present Church Edifice at Eightieth Street and Lexington Avenue. Photo: Sigurd Fischer.

Preface

This is the third and last volume of a trilogy on the history of the Unitarian movement in New York City, with special emphasis upon the history of the Unitarian Church of All Souls. The first volume, *Liberals Among the Orthodox: Unitarian Beginnings in New York City, 1819-1839,* covered the initial 20-year period from the founding of the church in 1819 through the ministry of William Ware, and the brief but troubled ministry of Dr. Charles Theodore Christian Follen. The second volume, Henry Whitney Bellows, covered the period of Bellows' life from his birth in 1814 until his death in 1882, the last 43 years of which he was the minister of All Souls Church. This was the first biography of Henry Bellows to be written. Bellows was one of the strongest churchmen of the Unitarian denomination. This third volume continues the history of the church, from Bellows death in 1882, until the end of my ministry in 1978.

In writing history some time should elapse so that events and ideas can be seen with some perspective. Some of the events during my ministry, 1955-1978, I think can now be seen with some perspective. But when one tries to write the history of current events, one only truly tries to write about things as they have occurred. So in writing about most of the period of my ministry, I am not pretending to write history in the usual manner that I could in Volumes I and II, or even the earlier chapters of this volume. But it seemed to me to be unfair to the present not to at least relate these events, and to let them take their place in history.

One will almost immediately notice a difference in tone of the events in this volume as compared to the events and ideas in Volumes I and II. From 1819 through Bellows' time many of the events which happened in the churches influenced strongly events in the country. The Pilgrims who landed at Plymouth Rock were radicals in religion in that they were outside of the Church of England. And the Puritans who came eight years later to Salem and then to Boston also had tried to "purify" the established Church of England, but their presence was not tolerated in England. Their ideas, as those of the Pilgrims, were very influential in the making of the American philosophy and spirit of government. They brought notions of democratic government which eventually found their lodging in the congregational form of church government, in the American Declaration of Independence, especially the Bill of Rights which was added to the Constitution several years later. These ideas of democracy were bred in the churches. The ideas of the Puritans affected American thought and morals far more than many realize.

We shall be introduced to some important figures in this volume. But somehow the scenery seems to have changed. No one person or set of persons carries the weight that they did in the other volumes. Of course, there were many more Americans in 1900 than in 1800. And fewer individuals as time went on were able to have the influence of a Bellows.

I am indebted to many persons for help in writing this last volume. Dr. Church and his ministerial colleagues at All Souls, Rev. John Buehrens and Rev. Richard Leonard have been most helpful, as has the whole staff at the church. Mrs. Angie Utt, who has worked as a volunteer with the historical material, has been particularly helpful. The All Souls Historical Society which was formed after I retired, has done a masterful job in getting all of the historical materials of the church together in an orderly way.

I am indebted to Alan Seaberg, curator of manuscripts at Andover Harvard Library, who introduced me as a one-day-a-week volunteer for three years, into cataloguing manuscripts, including the Presidential Papers of Dr. Samuel Atkins Eliot, Dr. Frederick May Eliot, and the correspondence of the Department of the Ministry of the American Unitarian Association. I owe a debt of gratitude to my wife who has always encouraged me to finish this book when my enthusiasm waned, as it often did.

I am especially indebted to Carl Seaburg who has edited all three volumes of this trilogy. His knowledge of Unitarian and Universalist history made him more than just an editor. His wise counsel pervades the series, and he has been able to tie the three books together so that they truly form a trilogy.

James Sutton, the librarian of the Morse Institute in Natick was helpful, as well as several of the presidents of the board of trustees of All Souls who continually prodded me to finish this last volume. Above all I am grateful that a project begun in 1965 with a study of the history of the church is now completed a quarter of a century later.

June 1991.   Walter Donald Kring
                                              Brookfield, Massachusetts

Prologue

The First Congregational Church of New York City (later to be called All Souls) had been founded by a group of laymen after a visit to New York City by William Ellery Channing of Boston in 1819. Channing was on his way to Baltimore to preach what later came to be known as "The Baltimore Sermon." On the basis of Scripture Channing challenged the Calvinistic doctrine of the more conservative Congregational churches to show that belief in the Unitarian view that God was one and not a trinity of Gods was sanctioned by the Scriptures. On the return to Boston he again stopped to visit his sister in New York, and this time he preached three times at the Hall of the Medical College in Barclay Street. The result of this visit was the formation of the First Congregational Church in the City of New York. This name was chosen because it was possible to incorporate under this denomination in the state of New York. The new congregation wanted Dr. Channing to be their minister, but he refused, as did John Brazer.

Finally, the choice to be the first pastor fell on another young man trained for the ministry at Harvard, William Ware, younger brother of Henry Ware Jr. and the son of Henry Ware whose appointment as a liberal theological professor at Harvard had caused such a great controversy in 1805. William Ware served the church faithfully for fifteen years from 1821 until 1836. But he was always unsure that he was an adequate preacher, and later in life he turned to writing for a livelihood. He wrote some history of the Unitarian movement, and he also wrote a series of historical novels set in the time of the Roman Empire which earned him a niche in American literature.

His place was filled temporarily by Charles Theodore

Christian Follen, a refugee from Germany and something of a Transcendentalist. But his thick German accent and some of his liberal political ideas did not please the congregation. He preached for two years, but the congregation never offered him a call to the pulpit, and he left New York to found and to design and build his own church in Lexington in 1838.(1)

The second installed minister of the church was Henry Whitney Bellows. This great churchman was the minister of All Souls for forty-three years.(2)

Dr. Bellows was probably the greatest churchman ever produced by the Unitarian denomination. When he died on January 31, 1882, he died at the height of his powers. He had been the minister of All Souls Church all his life. Not only had he been the able leader of his own church in a great and growing city, but he had led the Unitarians into organizing the only effective denominational structure they had up until this time with the National Conference of Unitarian Churches. He had the support, as no one else, of the various segments within the often warring factions of the denomination. He had been a moderating influence among his colleagues.

Although Bellows was considered a religious conservative by his fellow ministers, it was he who believed that a national church could be formed incorporating the disparate elements of the denomination. He was what was called a "Broad Churchman," in that he believed that all persons did not have to think alike in order to worship together or to form a national denomination. It was Bellows who tried to secure an invitation for the Universalists to attend the National Conference of Unitarian Churches convention in New York City in April 1865. He did not succeed in this because of pressure from the laymen of the denomination many of whom having come recently to Unitarianism felt that the addition of Universalism would only be confusing.

In addition to his churchly duties, Henry Bellows played a large role on the national scene. He helped to organize and was the president of the United States Sanitary Commission, the Red Cross of the Civil War. He knew almost everyone in Washington and in government circles. It was the women of New York City who began the Sanitary Commission, but they turned to Dr. Bellows for leadership because he was an astute organizer. He and a committee went to Washington to try to persuade the army that sanitary conditions were needed in the military camps which were rapidly being filled with volunteers who thronged to Washington to defend the capital. The United States Sanitary Commission ministered to the needs of the soldiers directly on the battlefields of that bloody war. It also ministered to them once they were mustered out. The Sanitary Commission went directly to the battlefields after a battle with their wagon trains carrying medical supplies, clothing, and food for the troops. Their work was so successful that the army eventually adopted their patterns and incorporated many of their methods into the Army Medical Corps. It was not until the year of Bellows' death that the United States finally joined the International Red Cross movement, led by a Universalist named Clara Barton.(3)

When the funeral of Henry Bellows took place on February 2, 1882, the church was filled with dignitaries from many walks of life. Edward Everett Hale tried to sum up in his funeral sermon the qualities and the contributions of his dear friend. After the funeral service, the family embarked by rail for Walpole, New Hampshire, where Bellows was buried in the family plot, near his father, his mother, and his first wife, Eliza Townsend Bellows. The family returned sadly to New York City.

Almost immediately the congregation of All Souls was involved in practical matters. They met in the parish house on Tuesday evening, February 14, 1882, and adopted a resolution appreciation for the life and work of their leader of forty-three years. The long resolution which they adopted spoke of "the disinterested labors and public usefulness of our late minister." The congregation praised his "strong, prolific, versatile intellect, his wonderful command of select and appropriate language, his occasional and extempore addresses, his Christian fellowship unhedged by creed or caste, his practical example of devotion to duty." They spoke of Henry Bellows' "courage and unflinching persistence in whatever cause he espoused, his nobility and grandeur of soul, his almost feminine tenderness of heart;" and they expressed sympathy to his bereaved family.(4)

A similar resolution from the Second Church in New York (The Church of the Messiah, now the Community Church)(5), and a resolution from the Church of the Savior in Brooklyn were also read at the meeting, and recorded in the minute book in beautifully inscribed letters.(6) The congregation also voted to pay Bellows' salary to his young widow through the first of April, and to pay all of the funeral expenses.

The Christian Register, the weekly newspaper of the denomination, contained many articles and expressions of respect for Dr. Bellows. The issue of February 2, 1882, (the day of the funeral) had an article on "The Fallen Cedar," and the funeral oration of Edward Everett Hale was printed in full. The next issue on February 9, had a more complete account of the funeral and the graveside service in Walpole. The next issue of February 16, contained an article about Bellows by John White Chadwick. The issue of February 28, contained many tributes to Bellows. *Leslie's Illustrated Newspaper* in its edition of February 11, printed an engraving of Dr. Bellows and an account of his life. All over the country obituary notices appeared in the local papers, testifying that Bellows was indeed a figure of national importance.

If the world in general took a long time to get used to the fact that Bellows was gone, the church itself had to be more concerned with caring for the living rather than grieving for the dead. The congregation turned immediately to the practical duty of provid ing some income for the young widow and her three young children. At the age of sixty, Henry Bellows, a widower, had married the daughter of the former minister of King's Chapel in Boston, the late Rev. Ephraim Peabody, Ellen Peabody. They had three children in the eight years of their marriage, the youngest, Ellen, being only two when her father died. The congregation set about raising the sum of $50,000 which was used to buy an annuity for Mrs. Bellows and the children. It is difficult to imagine the magnitude of this sum in our times, but it was a significant gift then. With Bellows drawing a salary of $10,000 a year it is some times difficult for us to understand why Bellows died with almost no financial resources. The money that was left in Bellows' will was money that had come to him through his first wife, Eliza Townsend, who at the time of their marriage was the daughter of the richest member of All Souls. The money necessarily went to the two surviving children of that marriage, Russell Nevins Bellows and Anna Bellows. Neither Russell nor Anna had been conspicuous money-earners during the lifetime of their father, and he had supported them along with his new family. In addition, the Bellows' had always lived very well, and had spent money as freely as they received it. The widow of Dr. Bellows obviously needed financial help to raise her young children, and the congregation responded graciously and generously.

So at the end of 63 years, the congregation of All Souls had been served by two ministers (Ware and Bellows), with one other minister (Follen) serving somewhat as an interim between them. In that time the church had become firmly established and proved to have a significant voice in the denomination and the nation.

*Theodore Chickering Williams: Third Minister of All Souls
(1883-1896)*

CHAPTER 1

A Poet At Heart:

The Ministry of Theodore Chickering Williams (1883-1896)

The desire to do good to others is indeed a stirring of what is highest in our natures and a reflection in us of the divine love itself. But you often need to remember that the greatest service you can render to a fellow creature is to show him what in your soul is best and "likest God'" and so bring him the help and inspiration of a higher life."(1)
Theodore Chickering Williams

With the death of Bellows, the congregation was faced with the difficult task of filling the pulpit with a successor. He had been such a powerful preacher and leader, and he had been at All Souls so long, that it seemed impossible to find anyone who could fill his shoes. Naturally, the congregation wanted a clone of the young Bellows when he had come to All Souls in 1839. This being impossible, they still began their search on a note of optimism. But they soon discovered that many of the leaders of the denomination were not enthusiastic about taking their friend's place in New York City. Dr. Hale did remain in New York City after the funeral service and preached the following Sunday. Reverend Robert Collyer of the Church of the Messiah preached the following Sunday, and Dr. Willian Henry Furness of Philadelphia, the next Sunday.

The list of those who filled the pulpit while the congregation was getting used to the fact that Bellows was actually gone

included Joseph May of Philadelphia, Francis Greenwood Pea-
body (Bellows' brother-in-law) of Cambridge. Two men named
Bellows also preached, Reverend John A. Bellows of Waterville,
Maine, and Bellows' son, Reverend Russell N. Bellows.

Searching for a Successor

None of these men had been considered to be a candidate for
minister of the church. So much time had passed without much
happening that the congregation decided to wait until after the
summer vacation to choose a pastor. But they did set up a procedure for hearing candidates. The procedure was quite simple;
two of the trustees were to go to a minister's own church, hear
him preach on his home ground, and then make a recommendation to the congregation. To speed up this process, the president
of the board of trustees of the church, Harsen Rhoades, suggested
at a June meeting of the society that they would probably select
several candidates and let the congregation hear them in the fall
and winter. This democratic procedure was unusual for the times.
Then a minister was often selected by the trustees of a church
without the approval of the congregation until everything had
been settled. Over the next few months, the congregation took
many formal and informal votes on a variety of candidates.

By the time the congregation had heard all of them, they
met on January 3, 1883 to proceed to the election of a minister.
Bellows had been in his grave for almost eleven months by this
time. At this meeting, Francis Greenwood Peabody emerged as
the top choice with 30 votes. Theodore Chickering Williams of
Winchester, Massachusetts, had 25 votes, and B.F. Hornbrooke of
Newton, Massachusetts, had 20 votes. On a second vote Peabody
was still in the lead, but Hornbrooke moved into second place, and
Williams into third place.

The pulpit was therefore offered to Reverend Francis Greenwood
Peabody, Bellows' own brother-in-law. But Peabody subsequently
wrote a letter to the congregation asking that he not be considered for

the pulpit, his stated reason being that his work in Cambridge was too important for him to consider a change.

One likes to surmise what would have happened at All Souls Church if a man of the stature of Francis Greenwood Peabody had accepted the post. Peabody had been born in Boston in 1847, the youngest child of Reverend Ephraim Peabody. He entered Harvard in the class of 1869, and was later graduated from the Harvard Divinity School in 1872. In 1874 he accepted the pastorate of the First Church in Cambridge, but resigned in 1879 due to ill health. He then lectured on homiletics at the Divinity School. President Charles W. Eliot was loathe to give his brother-in-law a place on the Harvard faculty for fear of being accused of nepotism, but Peabody was eventually appointed lecturer in ethics and homiletics for the year 1880-1881, and became the Parkman Professor of Theology the next year. It was at this stage of his career that he was invited to fill the All Souls pulpit. One can understand his reluctance to move away from Cambridge. In 1886 he became Plummer Professor of Christian Morals, and remait in this professorship until 1913. He was the Dean of the Faculty of the Divinity School from 1901-1905. He was a particularly persuasive preacher, and one can readily understand why All Souls placed such a priority on securing him to succeed Dr. Bellows. But they ultimately failed to persuade him to leave Cambridge.

On January 16, 1883, the congregation met again, and after the letter from Francis Greenwood Peabody was read in which he declined the pulpit, they proceeded to vote formally and informally. These informal votes were a way to get the expression of the opinions of the women of the church, for according to state law women could not vote in legal meetings of the congregation until the 1920's. The first vote showed Williams and Hornbrooke tied with 35 votes each. The legal members (the men) then voted, and Hornbrooke received 27 votes, Edward Everett Hale received 19 votes, and Williams had 16 votes. It was moved to call Mr. Hornbrooke. But the by-laws of the church called for a three-quarters plurality which he had not received. In the formal ballot which followed, Hornbrooke had 41 votes, Williams 9, and Hale 2. Harsen Rhoades moved that the call be made unanimous, but as in many Unitarian meetings there were two dissenting votes. Still the three-quarters plurality had been obtained. William B. Prichard and Harsen Rhoades met with Rev. Hornbrooke at his residence in Newton, Massachusetts, and presented him with a formal call from the society. Mr. Hornbrooke was not nearly a man of the professional stature of Francis Greenwood Peabody, and he surprised the New York delegation by declining the call. He gave his reasons in a letter dated February 5, 1883: "My present parish has within a year built a beautiful and costly place of worship. . . the parish itself is in a formative condition, and many felt that my present withdrawal might be harmful to the growth of Liberal Christianity."(2)

Williams Is Called

On May 30, 1883, another meeting of the society was held. The trustees had called this special meeting to report an interview which they had had with Rev. Theodore Chickering Williams at Winchester, Massachusetts, who was the next candidate on the list. Mr. Williams had only recently been installed in the Winchester church, and the trustees wanted congregational permission to write to the Winchester church for permission to call their minister. The meeting gave the necessary authority to call Mr. Williams. The trustees wrote to the Winchester society: "He has come to you too recently and your claims upon him are too strong to allow us to urge him to leave you unless you freely tell us that we may do so."(3) Such a procedure when a large church wanted to call are cently settled minister from a smaller church was considered the polite and orderly thing to do. One asks what kind of a response was expected by the New York church except to go ahead. All Souls had been in somewhat the same position itself, when in1864 after the death of Thomas Starr King, the San Francisco church had asked to "borrow" Dr. Bellows for six months.(4)

The Winchester society obligingly replied: "We relinquish any claim that we may have or may be supposed to have on Mr. Williams as our pastor."(5) A call was extended to Theodore Chickering Williams, and the trustees wrote to him:

> *"We decide once more to take for our leader and standard bearer another almost equally young man in years {referring to Bellows' coming to New York in his mid-twenties} and experi ence, asking him to take this church and we, its people, to be come our spiritual teacher, our guide, and our friend, to share our joys, as he must share our griefs, and more than all to hold us fast to those precious truths which for so many years have been taught from this pulpit."(6)*

Williams accepted the call, adding this peculiar comment: "I gladly cooperate with you in your experiment of educating, or rather creating your future minister."(7)

Williams answer sounds somewhat ominous for the expectations of the New York church. Was Williams to lead, as the church obviously meant that he should, or was he to be a student?

Theodore Chickering Williams was born in Brookline, Massachusetts, on July 2, 1855. His father, Frederick J. Williams, was a civil engineer and a man of unusual refinement who had a broad range of interests in his reading. Williams' own interest in books and literature, which was one of the dominating influences of his life, obviously owed much to the example of his father. His delight in books and literature had also been stimulated by the headmaster of the Roxbury Latin School, W. C. Collar, where young Williams received his schooling. It was one of the best preparatory schools in the country, founded in 1645 by the Reverend John Eliot, emphasizing an education in the classics.

This education well prepared young Williams to enter Harvard College with the class of 1876. At the college in the atmosphere of a newly adopted elective system, his scholarly temperament and taste for literature enabled him to receive a fine education. Throughout his four years at Harvard, he was high in rank in scholarship, was elected a member of Phi Beta Kappa, and was chosen to be the

Class Day Orator. He was a genial young man, and was popular with his classmates, having been a member of the Institute of 1770 and the Hasty Pudding Club.

George Herbert Palmer who wrote an introduction to the Georgics and Ecologues of Virgil, which Williams later translated from the Latin, wrote of him that "he was of middle height, slight in figure, light-haired, with mobile, subtle features which imparted to his face an expression like that of Emerson or Cardinal Newman. His unusual powers of intellectual and moral leadership were early recognized."(8)

After graduation from Harvard and a year of teaching school, Williams returned to Cambridge to study for the ministry at the Harvard Divinity School. Here also he made his mark as a brilliant student. After three years at Harvard Divinity School he was called to the First Unitarian Society in Winchester, Massachusetts. He was ordained into the Unitarian ministry in 1882. A year later he married Verna Curtis Wright of Boston, with whom throughout his life he found perfect companionship. He had a happy but short ministry at Winchester, when All Souls Church, looking for another brilliant young Bellows, asked the Winchester church if they might "steal" their minister.

Theodore Williams with his young bride left Winchester for New York City for what he hoped would be a remarkable preach ing career. It had been a difficult decision to go to New York. One can imagine that there was a good deal of trepidation on his part as to whether his own internal nature, which was so different from that of the mature Bellows, could succeed in a large metropolis. His comment in his letter of acceptance that he was to be a student and the church members to be his teachers shows his own inner fears. But, on the other hand, he had obviously been chosen for this distinguished post because of his brilliance and his future promise.

The installation service for Theodore Williams was a model of simplicity. An original hymn for the occasion had been written by Rev. H. Price Collier. Rev. John White Chadwick, who had served the Brooklyn church for forty years, gave the opening prayer. The sermon significantly was given by Francis Greenwood Peabody, who had been the first choice of the congregation as their minister. The prayer of installation; was given by Rev. James Freeman Clarke, an old man at this time, and minister of the Church of the Disciples in Boston. The right hand of fellowship was given by Rev. Robert Collyer of New York's Church of the Messiah, and an address to the people was given by Rev. Edward Everett Hale of Boston. A more distinguished group of Unitarian ministers could hardly have been assembled in 1883, and their presence indicated the hopes that the Unitarian ministry had for a significant career for young Theodore Chickering Williams.

Early Years at All Souls

When Theodore Williams first came to New York City, *The New York Tribune,* in an article titled "The Youthful Pastor in the Pulpit," said of him:

> *The successor of Dr. Bellows seems strongly antithetical in personality, purposes, and professional equipment. He is almost a youth, not yet thirty. He has been a licensed preacher hardly two years. He is slight of frame. He has a delicate light voice, and speaks under some physical constraint. There is nothing astonishing or masterly on the surface of his ministrations.*

But the article continued with some friendlier words;

> *He is transferred to the metropolitan church of his denomination and stands in the place of an acknowledged orator and master among his fellows. At first glance the All Souls' people seem to have weakly fallen in with the present indiscriminate craze for young ministers. But it needs little consideration to vindicate the essential wisdom and soundness of this selection. For Mr. Williams at the outset is a pastor who will feed well the flock in his own fold before he spends*

his fodder at large. He will deal with individuals rather
than masses - will manipulate only so far as he first reaches
and ministers to individual lives.(9)

This newspaper article could hardly have been called "A good press." But it illustrates the ambiguous attitude that many persons must have had about a young and untried minister attempting to fill the rather large shoes of Henry Whitney Bellows.

Fortunately, many in the church found in Williams only the youth of the young Bellows. In many ways he was the antithesis of everything that had made Bellows such a famous minister, churchman, and public figure. He was obviously not going to lead the church in the same way that Bellows had. But the church and the congregation had also changed over the long years of Bellows' ministry. The congregation had been aging, and many of the important members of the church had died. Their places had not been filled with people of equal renown or financial means. The church must have hoped that Williams would devote his energies to rebuilding All Souls rather than attaining the prominence that Bellows had.

Problems: Financial and Otherwise

Although the church took advantage of Williams' youth and offered him a salary of $6,000 a year, rather than the $10,000 that Bellows had drawn, they still had financial problems. There was also a good deal of discussion about the Sunday School and where it ought to meet. The attached building at the rear of the church had served originally as the home of the minister, as a church parlor, and as a meeting-place for the Sunday School. From the point of view of the Sunday School it was a badly designed building. Bellows had continually complained about the parsonage, and finally in despair moved out and bought his own home nearby. Williams followed Bellows' example and secured his own lodgings, and the parsonage became the home of the sexton, in a New York

City church a very dignified and honorable position. In those days a sexton often doubled as the undertaker for the congregation thus adding to his income. The sexton was not considered a janitor but a manager of the church property, and often he hired assistants to do the difficult cleaning and maintenance work in the church.

The interior of All Souls about 1891. Note the elaborate sounding board over the pulpit to aid the acoustics.

During Williams' ministry there were few major changes. One of the minor changes was moving the communion service to an afternoon hour. There were also some serious acoustical problems in the church in spite of the fact that a sounding board had been installed behind the pulpit in Bellows' time. Theodore Williams had been an orator both at college and the Divinity School, but surprisingly the acoustics of the church which had sufficed for Bellows did not prove capable of projecting Williams' voice so that he could be adequately heard. It is well to remember that this third All Souls' building was a basilica with heavy stone and brick walls, and the echo problem must have been a hard one for the person who was speaking. The trustees tried all kinds of experiments with the acoustics. But the problem came back to the fact that Williams simply did not have the strength of voice that Bellows had.

There is also another factor not usually considered in church acoustics. Bellows usually preached to a full or nearly full house. This probably made the acoustics much better in this cathedral like building. Williams did not command the national prominence and attention that Bellows did, and the Sunday morning congregation became smaller and smaller, which certainly must have discouraged the young man for the acoustics became worse as the crowds grew smaller. There are certain churches that are popular with visitors to New York City. Bellows commanded such an audience. Theodore Williams did not.

An Assistant Minister

During the years of Mr. Williams' ministry the church made its first experiment of having a full-time minister in charge of the Sunday School. In 1888, a Mr. Waller was asked to reorganize and be in charge of the Sunday School. Then it was agreed that a full time assistant minister could both run the Sunday School and help Mr. Williams. Mr. Goddard headed a group of parishioners who guaranteed the sum of $2,000 a year for five years to conduct the experiment. Rev. Charles F. Russell was called to the position, but declined the offer.

In September 1889, Mr.Williams recommended a man who seemed to be eminently suited to All Souls, William Ware Locke. He had, of course, been named in honor of the first minister of the church, William Ware. He accepted the call, but after one year resigned. Whether the women's charities, which he was supposed to oversee, or the Sunday School children were too rambunctious for him, we do not know. By the following September Mr. Locke had been replaced by Reverend Frederick J. Gault. But he lasted for only two years before he resigned, giving as his reason that he found it impossible to work with The Friendly Aids, one of the charitable organizations associated with the church. Thus ended the experiment to have an assistant minister run the Sunday School and do some supervision of associated organizatoin.

Not Another Bellows

Obviously the church had chosen a different type of man than Henry Bellows. Bellows had been constantly on the move, working relentlessly for social reforms in the New York community and the nation, writing sermons on trains, and traveling all over the country for important engagements. He had an almost inexhaustible supply of physical energy. Williams, on the other hand, was quiet and retiring. He also had health problems. His life was divided into segments when his health was good and segments when it was poor. In the final analysis, Theodore Williams was more of a poet and a writer of hymns than an activist in society. Perhaps more than anything else his study of the classics at the Roxbury Latin School and at Harvard endeared ancient Roman and Greek literature to him. He later made an excellent translation of Vergil's *Aeneid,* and Tibullus' *Elegies.*

But what Theodore Williams lacked in active qualities were more than supplied in full measure by his wife, Velma Curtis Wright Williams. She organized the New York League of Unitarian Women, and later established Senexet House near Putnam, Connecticut, after her husband's death, which has flourished as a retreat house for many church-related groups. She gave valuable help to her husband in the compilation of a hymnbook titled *Amore Dei,* which for some years was used at All Souls. They made an excellent team in the ministry of the church.

This joint effort in hymnody was completed by Theodore and Velma Williams in May of 1890 when George H. Ellis of Boston published their new hymnal *Amore Dei.* It is a small hymnbook of slightly over two hundred pages which contains 382 hymns and over twenty chants and responses. Dr. Henry Wilder Foote states that "while still a student in the Harvard Divinity School (Theodore Williams) wrote one of the best ordination hymns in the language, and, in later years, eight others, still in use, which are religious poetry of a high order."(10) Velma Williams was a compiler, she wrote no hymns. In the "Preface" to *Amore Dei,* Williams states that "Hymns. . . are not written for speech but for song." There was an attempt to avoid formalism, and especially emphasized was the blending of words with music. Theodore Williams said of the volume that "It is eminently fitted for family use, and I believe that in the larger circle of the Christian congregation, it cannot fail to bring joy, beauty, fervor into the service of sacred song."

The hymnal was obviously used at All Souls, perhaps as a second hymnal, for the copy of the hymnbook in the church archives has printed on its cover in gold leaf, "Church of All Souls." How long the hymnbook was used is not known, but a second edition was published in 1897. Dr. Foote states that "it was used in many other churches as well."(11) But as the twentieth century progressed there was a reaction against the sentimentalism which Theodore Williams represented, and just as his own hymns were used less and less in successive hymbooks put out by the Unitarians, so was the use of hymnals of which the Williams hymnbook is representative.

Surprisingly, there are only 6 hymns and a translation by Williams. In the biographical index of authors, Williams entry is very modest, "A Unitarian minister, graduate from Harvard University, 1876, and Cambridge Divinity School, now minister of All Souls Church, New York City."

We might recall that this was the second hymnbook that was put out by those closely associated with the church. In 1820, even before the original parish had called William Ware to be their minister, they expressed a desire for a hymnbook that was not of a sectarian nature. Henry Devereux Sewall came forward with a collection of the words to hymns which he had collected, some from contemporary sources. It was adopted by the Society. It appeared early in 1821, and was called *A Collection of Psalms and Hymns,* but it is better known as "The New York Collection" or the Sewall Hymnal. In his modesty, Henry Sewall never put his name on the book. It is interesting especially because Sewall took some liberties in changing the words to some poems submitted by William Cullen Bryant, an early associate of the church, and not yet famous.(12)

In 1886, a life-sized bas-relief of Dr. Bellows which had been commissioned from Augustus Saint-Gaudens was unveiled in the church with special ceremonies. Theodore Chickering Williams gave the dedicatory address. Remarks were also made by Robert Collyer, Horatio Stebbins, and Edward Everett Hale. Francis Greenwood Peabody gave the prayer, and the words on the memorial were written by President Charles W. Eliot of Harvard University. The unveiling was done by Henry Bellows' two sons; Henry Bellows, Jr, aged eleven, and Robert Peabody Bellows, aged nine.(13)

In 1888, Theodore Williams was elected to the honorable position of a member of the Board of Preachers of Harvard University. Under this obligation he preached several time a year at the University until 1890. In these years he also began to take a more active part in the annual meetings of the society. The first reference in the church minute books to a woman performing an official act appears in the church minutes in January 1892 when Edith Cornell made a motion at the annual meeting.

Herman Melville's Membership

During the writing of volume II of the History of All Souls, *Henry Whitney Bellows,* it was established that Herman Melville was a bona-fide member of All Souls Church. All of the photographic evidence for this was published in 1981 by the Melville Society in a small 80-page book, *The Endless, Winding Way in Melville: New Charts by Kring and Carey,* edited by Donald Yannella and Hershel Parker. The book contains photos of all the All Souls records which establish this fact; Melville's name as it appears in the treasurer's pew record book, 1850; the record of his daughter, Elizabeth Shaw Melville's baptism on March 31, 1872; Melville's name and address, as it appears in Theodore Williams' membership book, circa 1884; the record of Melville's funeral service conducted on September 28, 1891 by Mr. Williams at the Melville home at East 26th Street; and the pathetic letter of Elizabeth Melville to Mr. Prichard, the church treasurer, December 31, 1872, indicating that they could no longer afford the pew rent of $22 per year. The members of the Melville Society were so surprised that Herman Melville had been a Unitarian that they issued this booklet so that these records would be safely kept. Thus, this information can be found in the libraries of Melville scholars around the world.

Henry Bellows was a very poor record keeper, and the list of church members which he was supposed to keep has never turned up either in the church records or in the Bellows Papers at the Massachusetts Historical Society. So we may never know exactly when Herman Melville went to his minister and told him that he wished to be listed as a member of the church. Melville's name does appear in Theodore Chickering Williams' membership book which he gathered together shortly after he became the minister of the church in 1883. This was not a signed membership book, but a record kept by the pastor. The church By-Laws stated that anyone could become a member of the church (as opposed to owning or renting a pew) if he presented himself before the minister and asked to become a member.(13) Perhaps Melville never joined the church under Bellows, but became interested in the church when a fellow poet and writer became the minster. It is very likely that the Melville family attended church as is wit- nessed by the hymn book with the Melville name on it which is kept at "Arrowhead," Melville's home while he lived in Pittsfield, Massachusetts, for thirteen years between 1850 and 1863.

At the time that Theodore Williams became the minister of All Souls, Herman Melville was writing a great deal of poetry. In 1876 he had published one of the longest and most obscure poems in the English language, the massive *Clarel*, and he wrote poetry and the short novel *Billy Budd,* late in his life. Theodore Williams was also a poet and a writer of hymns. I like to surmise that these two poets got along well together, and that at this time Melville indicated to Williams that he wished to join the church. The By-Laws state: "All those who considered themselves members of the church shall be required to inform the pastor of this fact & all those who propose uniting with is shall previously signify it to the pastor - that he may enter their names upon the church records."(14) This was the very broad basis of membership when Herman Melville first rented a pew in 1849, and when he joined the church, probably when Theodore Williams was the minister.

I researched this matter at length because some of the finest Melville scholars just don't believe that Melville ever joined any church. They think he might have gone to church with "Lizzie" occasionally, but the fact that church membership required a person to go to the minister puts a more serious light upon this subject.

One unfortunate matter is that the papers of Theodore Williams, having been passed from one member of the family to another over the years, were finally judged to be worthless and were destroyed. Williams was the minister of All Souls for eight years before Herman Melville died. The funeral service was conducted in Melville's home at East 26th Street, just six blocks north of All Souls Church, on September 28, 1891. It was undoubtedly held in the home rather than the church because Melville had become a recluse, and when he passed away, the New York newspapers scarcely took cognizance of the fact that one of the most gifted American literary figures had died. His fame was to come early in the twentieth century. The church would have been too large for such an "unimportant" figure, and the attendance at the home was small.

Resignations

On February 6, 1896, Rev. Frederick J. Gault resigned from the position of assistant minister at All Souls Church. He stated in a letter to Warren N. Goddard, the president of the board of trustees, "The relations between us has been most cordial and sympathetic." He especially appreciated "the generous helpful friendship of Mr. and Mrs. Williams." He had evidently had troubles running his assigned job with the Friendly Aid Society. He believed that this work could be better carried on by "someone more suited, one who can make it his supreme interest." But he wanted not a specialized pastorate but "to enter upon the duties of the regular ministry as the pastor of a parish." The Board accepted his resignation as of the first of March as he had requested.(15)

The church minutes do not suggest that there is any relationship between Rev. Gault's letter of resignation, and the letter which was dated March 5, a month later, addressed to the board of trustees. It was from Theodore Chickering Williams, and he too wished to resign from his duties at All Souls, to be effective in May or June. These two resignations, coming so close together suggest that there may have been further problems than just the Friendly Aid Society. Theodore Chickering Williams' reasons were given in his letter of resignation.

My reasons. . . for going away lie chiefly in myself. In order to increase my future usefulness as a Christian Minister, I feel that I need first a year's study without a parish, and, after that, an other charge.

I have not come to this conclusion quickly nor in any passing mood of fatigue but from an abiding sense of an intellectual and spiritual need.(16)

Mr. Williams had stated that he was going to convey this message to the congregation the following Sunday. So the Board of Trustees took no action except to call a meeting of the congregation for the evening of March 18, and the secretary was instructed to send such notices to all members through the mail.(17)

The congregational meeting was called to order by S. Sidney Smith of the standing committee. Hon. Dorman B. Eaton, a prominent lawyer and now a judge, was elected chairman. Mr. L. T. Russell then offered a resolution which very simply requested the trustees to arrange the date of Mr. Williams' resignation and "to make the proper provision for the supply of the pulpit and the discharge of pastoral functions until a successor to Mr. Williams can be selected and enter upon the discharge of his duties." A committee was appointed by the chair "to draw up resolutions expressing the deep sense of our loss in terms which shall do full justice to the affectionate sentiments of the congregation." They were to confer with Mr. Williams with a view to finding out if his resignation is irrevocable or whether we may hope for his return after a prolonged vacation, and that the result of their labors be submitted to the congregation at their next meeting."(18)

Surprisingly this last resolution, although accepted as an amendment by Mr. Goddard, lost by a vote of 39 to 37. The majority of the parish did not want Mr. Williams to reconsider his resignation. The idea of a vacation rather than termination of the pastorate did not seem appropriate to the majority. This would seem to indicate that there were some deeper problems than just a desire of the minister wishing to have a year of study. The fact that Theodore Williams suggested that "someone else" might better serve the church indicates that there were rumblings. We must remember that neither Mr. nor Mrs. Williams were at this meeting. And the small number of votes represents only the males present, as that was the voting custom at that time.

To supplant the lost motion, it was then moved that the resignation be accepted, and that the chair appoint a committee of three with power to add to their numbers to draw up resolutions expressing the "the deep sense of loss in terms which shall do full justice to the affectionate sentiments of the congregation."(19) This motion was carried. Mr. Ewart was named a committee of one by the trustees at a later meeting on April 6 to confer with Mr. Williams and to arrange when his resignation would take effect, and Harsen Rhoades was appointed a committee of one to provide for the supply of the pulpit until the summer vacation.

A call was sent out for another congregational meeting to be held on April 8. The resolutions had been drawn up by the special committee and S. Sidney Smith read the resolution which in-printed form was distributed to the congregation. The resolution was in good spirits:

> *Thirteen years of association have endeared him to our hearts. . . . His pastorate has overflowed with spiritual help-fulness to each one of us individually, and in a wider sphere has been full of usefulness to this city. . . . a student by na-ture, his sermons and addresses have been, at all times, of a high intellectual order, marked {by} thoughtfulness, ear-nestness and felicitous expression. . . . Always abreast of the thought of the day, never faltering in his statements and defense of that form of religious belief, so precious and deep-rooted in this Society, he has been ever true to the best traditions of our faith."(20)*

Reasons Why

Shedding a good deal of light on Mr. Williams' resignation is a document in the All Souls archives, a letter from George R. Bishop dated in 1927, many years after the events, in which he explains what happened to Theodore Chickering Williams during his last few years at All Souls. He mentions that Williams was "for a time popular, though he never developed talent for preaching and whatever may have been {expected.}" Williams had been at the head of his class at Harvard and had been an orator at the Divinity School. But Bishop states that he ever give enough preparation time to his preaching week after week. Williams told Mr. Bishop in 1895, his last full year at All Souls, that "often on Saturday mornings he would go to the Century (Club), select his topic and his text for the sermon of the next day." He often wrote the sermon at one sitting before going home for luncheon. Bishop wrote that "the result was inevitable." With this lack of sermon preparation, church attendance fell off and there were fewer pew owners and renters. "It was evident that All Souls faced disintegration and total collapse except the pastorate were changed."

According to Mr. Bishop there was a small following loyal to Mr. Williams which voted against the acceptance of Williams resignation. But eventually the majority accepted the resignation, and Mr. Bishop says "thus All Souls was saved."(21)

Perhaps in rebuttle to this rather grim picture of Theodore Williams' character are the words of one of his dear friends, Rev. Francis G. Peabody, D.O. of Harvard, who knew him intimately all of his life. "He had hard things to bear, but he was not hard ened by them. He had much to sober him, but remained playful and serene. He was, as another poet has said, one of those noble souls 'who conquer grief by dint of tending suffering not their own.'"

Dr. Palfrey Perkins later wrote of Williams' years in New York:

Here indeed was a trial of youthful strength. For thirteen years, Theodore Chickering Williams met the challenge with all of the winning and magnetic qualities of his spirit. Having the simplicity of a poet and the depths of a philosopher, his preaching made a lasting impression not only on his congregation, but upon the larger life of the great city.(22)

Again, putting it kindly, Williams was undoubtedly a fish out of water in the hectic life of New York City, which is scarcely the place for a poet and a dreamer to flourish, particularly if he is managing a congregation of people driven by ambition and in some cases, greed. His failure to write sermons every week like an automaton must have been due to his poetic instincts. He didn't write poetry by sitting down with a blank piece of paper at a given time and composing a poem. He was inspired to write a poem or a hymn. It was not his manner to arrange to be inspired every week-end on schedule.

After All Souls

Theodore and Velma Williams went to Europe for two years of rest and recuperation. Upon his return Williams spent a year in Oakland, California, supplying the pulpit of the Unitarian Church. At about this time plans were being formulated by Mrs. Caleb B. Hackley to establish a preparatory school at Tarrytown, New York, up the Hudson River from New York City. Mrs. Hackley, a New York City Unitarian, had been most generous in her gifts enthusiastically to the invitation to become the first headmaster. His scholarly interests and his appealing personality made him a logical choice.

During the five years that Williams served as the Hackley School's headmaster he showed a remarkable ability to head an educational institution. Palfrey Perkins wrote of Williams' achieve ents: "Hackley School today owes much of the beauty of its setting and eqmpment, as well as its traditions of scholarship and character, to the personal influence of its first headmaster."(23)

When he was forced to resign as Headmaster at Hackley School, Williams blamed Mr. Slicer, his successor at All Souls, who was on the Hackley Board, and at one time he threatened to return tlive in New York City. George Bishop goes on, in the letter previouly mentioned, to say that Mr. Williams wanted to make it difficult for Mr. Slicer when he came to All Souls. Mr. Bishop even quotes several conversations with Dr. Minot Savage, then the minster of the Church of the Messiah, saying that Williams told him he wished to make trouble.

In 1907, Mr. Williams went back to his first alma mater and served for two years as the headmaster of the Roxbury Latin School. But he again had one of his occasional bouts with illness and he was compelled to resign. In 1911, Western Reserve University in Cleveland, Ohio, conferred on Theodore Williams the honorary degree of Doctor of Letters (Litt.D.) He died on May 6, 1915.

Assessing Williams

Palfrey Perkins wrote of him: "He touched everything - his work, his play, his human relationships - with a creative hand and heart, so that he is remembered and honored as one who made of life itself a fine art."(24) If the author of this history believed in the transmigration of souls, he would have a good case, because I was born on March 10, 1916, just ten months after Dr. Williams died. The first time I saw Dr. Williams' portrait at All Souls I thought that it was a picture of my own father.

George Herbert Palmer, the Harvard philosopher, wrote an introduction to Theodore Williams' translation of the *Georgics and Ecologues of Virgil* which was published shortly after Williams' death. In this biographical sketch, Palmer gives an analysis of the character of this third minister of All Souls Church.

His mind played upon almost every subject it touched. The many aspects which truth might assume, its shades, its contradictions even, delighted him. He would suddenly question one of his deepest beliefs and had small regard for formal consistency. Intellectual stagnation was abhorrent to him and impossible for anyone in his company. Both thought and utterance were perpetually fresh and highly individual. Yet the texture of his mind was firm and its idealistic convictions seemed strengthened by continual criticism. The casual stranger felt that keen, original, and scholarly intellect which allowed itself no lazy ambiguities and was ever eager to receive greater reasonableness from others.(25)

Upon strict analysis it would seem that Theodore Williams was scarcely suited to the serious administrative and other problems of an urban ministry. Still, he did not have the intensity of doubt that plagued William Ware, the first minister of All Souls. But he was essentially an inward man by nature. This inner strength must have touched the lawyers, the bankers, and the merchants who dominated the membership of All Souls. Like all poets, he lived in the mood of the present, but like most poets his relationship with the present was not expressed in practical but in ideal and imagined terms.

Physically he was neither as strong nor as robust as Henry Bellows, who himself had health problems because he overdid, and over-tested his strength. While at All Souls he did several very significant things. While emerging from what was almost boyhood to manhood, he was able to meet the demands of a great city church. This is all the more surprising when one recalls that he had been in the ministry less than two years when he came to New York City. In the years that followed his resignation he proved himself to be an educator of no mean accomplishment, laying foundations for the eventual success of Hackley School and the Roxbury Latin School. Then after leaving the ministry and education, he proved himself to be a first-rate scholar turning to his first love, the poet Virgil.

Williams was a man of open-mindedness and keen intellectual refinement. He made poetry and the fine arts an ingredient of his daily life. He looked out onto the world almost with the eyes of a child, and tried to harmonize the discords with happy thoughts. He sometimes found it difficult to write, and simply could not write when he was not inspired. His religion was the religion of the inner life. He was a Unitarian of what might be called the conservative persuasion, but he was never led by his temperament into a lack of appreciation of other points of view. As George Herbert Palmer further said of him; "Whether teaching school, building a church, interpreting Virgil, or sitting as the scintillating center of a group of talkers, he was ever the Christian gentleman, dignified yet charming."(26) For thirteen years in New York City he met the challenge of a large city church with magnetic qualities of spirit.

The church erected in his honor a bas-relief depicting Dr. Williams working on a poem or words to a hymn, perhaps even writing a sermon, as a hovering angel offers inspiration and help across his shoulder. This bas-relief by Evelyn Beatrice Longman, and commissioned by Velma Williams, was completed in 1922, and placed in All Souls that year; and then moved to the present site in 1932 when the church moved north on the island of Manhattan and occupied its present building at Eightieth Street and Lexington Avenue.

Above all, Theodore Chickering Williams will be remembered as a writer of words for hymns. He was one of the great hymn writers in an age that produced many hymn writers of note; William Channing Gannett, Marion Franklin Ham, Frederick Lucian Hosmer, Samuel Longfellow, John Greenleaf Whittier, and many others. Unitarian and other hymnbooks contain his hymns. *The Hymn and Tune Book* of 1914 contained 19 hymns by Williams. *Hymns of the Spirit,* which appeared in 1937, contained the words to 11 hymns. The latest Unitarian hymnbook, *Hymns for the Celebration of Life,* published in 1964, contains only two. Here are the words to perhaps his most loved hymn.

When thy heart with joy o'er flowing,
Sings a thankful prayer.
In thy joy, O let thy brother
With thee share.

When the harvest sheaves ingathered,
Fill thy barns with store,
To thy God and to thy brother
Give the more.

If thy soul with power uplifted,
Yearns for glorious deed,
Give thy strength to serve thy brother
In his need.

Hast thou borne a secret sorrow
In thy lonely breast.
Take to thee thy sorrowing brother
In his need.

Share with him thy bread of blessing
Sorrow's burden share,
When thy heart enfolds a brother, God is there.

Rev. Dr. Theodore Chickering Williams died on May 6, 1915, and his burial service was held in King's Chapel the following Sunday afternoon. The service was in charge of Rev. Howard N. Brown, D.O., minister of King's Chapel, and Rev. Francis G. Peabody D.O. As a closing hymn the congregation sang "As the Storm Retreating" which was written by Mr. Williams. Internment was in Mount Auburn Cemetery in Cambridge. The ushers were Rev. Edward Everett Hale, Rev. Roderick Stebbins of Milton, Professor Henry W. Foote of the Harvard Divinity School, and Rev. Palfrey Perkins, later to be the minister of King's Chapel.

The Williams Memorial Plaque. Sculptor: Evelyn Beatrice Longman.

Thomas Roberts Slicer. Fourth Minister of All Souls (1897-1916)

One World At A Time

The Ministry of Thomas Roberts Slicer (1897-1916)

*"One World at a Time" is not in any sense to be construed
negatively. It affirms that "the life that now is," in the faith
that if the life that now is can be made strong and gracious
and full of delight, the suggestion that it will ever end will
be the last one the mind can be brought to entertain.(1)*

Thomas Roberts Slicer

After Theodore Williams had left the church on a trip to Europe, the preaching was done by substitutes. Many famous ministers were heard; such as Samuel A. Eliot, Edward Everett Hale, Minot Savage, Robert Collyer, John Carroll Perkins, William Wallace Fenn, Francis G. Peabody, Thomas R. Slicer, and Minot Osgood Simons. Meanwhile, the trustees were receiving suggestions for a new minister. Harsen Rhoades was in charge of the pulpit supply. On June 28 the church closed for the summer.

Slow Search for a Successor

Surprisingly, there is nothing in the Minute Book about a list of possible successors to Mr. Williams. The board of trustees did decide that the discussion of a successor was not in order for the annual meeting, but that a special meeting should be called for this purpose.

At the annual meeting on January 12, 1897, only routine matters were discussed. The treasurer's annual statement showed that for the past fiscal year disbursements had been about $23,000. The rate for taxation of the pews was kept at 22% on value of pews owned. and 26% on value of pews rented. This requires some explanation. Pews at All Souls were given a value when the church was first built, and then the pews were either owned or rented by the members of the congregation. The annual tax on the pews was figured from this original value, and members were assessed at an annual rate of either 22% if they owned the pew or 26% if they rented a pew.(2)

At the ensuing trustees meeting held on January 21, the main item of business was appointing a board of charities for the coming year. A board of nine persons was appointed. The name of Mrs. Frederick von Bernuth appears in the minutes for the first time. It was her will and the will of her sister which would bring the church's capital funds into so much better condition in 1956.

It was not until February 25 at a trustee's meeting that Mr. Rhoades stated that the main purpose of the meeting was to take steps for the choosing of a pastor. They decided to call the congregation together on March 9. At that time they wanted to test the personal preferences of all those who attended. They also wanted to ascertain if a pastor could be chosen without hearing any other ministers. Perhaps some of the famous preachers they had already heard were understood to be candidates. More probably some of the obscure ministers they had also heard were the likely candidates.

At the meeting it was moved to proceed to ballot to ascertain if the congregation was ready to select a minister without hearing any more candidates. This motion was carried. The congregation then proceeded to vote their preferences. Samuel Eliot received 25 votes, Dr. Slicer, 18 votes, Rev Augustus Lord, 5 votes, with several others receiving scattered votes. Then the congregation moved to an informal ballot. This was a way of getting the preferences of the women. Sixty-five votes were cast; Samuel Eliot received 29, Thomas Slicer received 29, and several others received a few votes. The meeting adjourned until March 23. The meeting held on the twenty-third was inconclusive and they adjourned once again to May 4.

To open the meeting on May 4, Daniel Davis read a list of the ministers who had preached at All Souls and who had agreed to preach again before July. Remarks were made by Hon. Dorman B. Eaton and Harsen Rhoades. Once again it was moved to adjourn for two weeks. Not only the pew holders but those who attended church regularly were to be invited to be present, and it was sug gested that if people could not attend that they should send prox ies. No progress towards the selection of a minister was being made fast.

Division in the Congregation

One reason for this temporizing may be explained by a letter in the church archives written by George R. Bishop on December 14, 1927. Bishop pointed out that there was still a small Theodore Williams' party in the congregation led by Sidney Smith, a trustee for many years. Bishop declared that the Sidney Smiths were do ing everything that they could to disrupt the church because their beloved Dr. Williams had been ousted.

Bishop wrote that the "Sidney Smiths would justify their own hostility to this chosen successor by sympathy on many points, with Mr. Williams, continued contact with whom they seemed to estimate as more valuable than any service and continuance of All Souls Church and Society."(3) He added that in regard to the ac ceptance of Theodore Williams resignation, that the Smiths pre ferred "the continuance of the man whose pastorate obviously was disastrous, and if continued likely soon to produce the complete disintegration of All Souls."(4)

At the meeting on May 18, a ballot had been prepared on which people were to list their preferences. The ballot was approved by the congregation, and finally voting took place. A motion was then made

"that the Trustees are authorized to select and report to

the Church for its approval a pastor from among the ministers thus voted for, the choice and report to be of the one who shall have received the greatest number of votes, unless he shall decline to become pastor in which event the one who has received the next largest number of votes who does not decline shall be selected and reported."(5)

This was carried. The meeting then voted that there be no announcement of the results of the ballot but that the ballots be referred to the trustees. Evidently the church was very divided on many issues. It had been over a year since Mr. Williams had resigned, and this was the first time that anything authoritative had been accomplished.

Slicer Is Chosen

The tellers reported to the trustees on May 24 that at the special meeting the greatest number of votes cast had been for Rev. Thomas R. Slicer. The trustees then decided to extend a call to the Rev. Thomas R. Slicer of Buffalo, New York. A committee of three trustees was to comprise a committee to tender a call to Mr. Slicer. This committee consisted of the chairman of the board of trustees, Harsen Rhoades, George R. Bishop, and Daniel A. Davis.

At the next meeting of the board on June 11, the chairman, Mr. Rhoades, reported that two trustees had arranged a meeting with Mr. Slicer in Boston at the rooms of the Unitarian Association on the previous Friday and Saturday. (Mr. Davis was absent.) They gave Mr. Slicer a cordial invitation to become the minister of All Souls Church. They even placed the balance sheets for the past four years in Mr. Slicer's hands so that he could study them. They offered him a salary of $5,000 explaining the difficult financial condition of the church. They met again that evening at the Hotel Brunswick at which time Mr. Davis was present. At this stage of the interview Mr. Slicer appeared to regard the invitation in "a favorable light provided all things worked out well with him and with his Society."

Meanwhile Slicer had considered the costs of living in New York City, and he informed the committee that he could not live on a salary of less than $8,000. He stated that he was not particularly interested in money, but that he had an obligation "if possible, to support himself and his family in a plain manner and upon a basis which would keep him free from debt."(6) The trustees agreed that they would extend themselves. He then asked that a formal letter be addressed to him and "that in that letter some appeal should be made to his Church, so as to induce good feeling on their part towards our Church, and possibly induce them from relinquishing their own claims in favor of our Church, and for the benefit of the cause at large."(7) Harsen Rhoades then read a draft of a formal letter.(8) In the letter the trustees spoke of the fact that the Buffalo church probably did not realize that the New York church had suffered a "decline in numbers" and had grown "weak in its power to uphold Unitarian Christianity in New York." They needed an energetic leader like Thomas Slicer and hoped that Buffalo would consider their request favorably.

In Buffalo, Slicer had been extremely active in both municipal and civil service reform work. When called to All Souls, he asked the if he could defer the beginning of his ministry until November, since he wanted to conclude an important campaign for reform in that city that was underway. His request was granted.

The board of trustees met again on June 25, and Harsen Rhoades was able to read a letter from Rev. Thomas Slicer formally accepting the call and expressing his appreciation of the kind way in which they had handled the rather sensitive matter of his Buffalo church's feelings. A printed note went out to the members of the congregation informing them of the events of the early summer. Dated July 1, the letter stated that due to the lateness of the season and the difficulty of getting enough of the congregation together during the summer months, it had been decided to wait until fall for the meeting of ratification by the society. This meet ing was held on October 21 and the board's choice was ratified. Mr. Slicer would begin his duties as the fourth "called" minister of All Souls on November first. The meeting of October 21 had some further business, the planning of a Conference of the Middle States and Canada which was to be held in All Souls Church during November. It was decided to have a separate meeting after the church service on Sunday October 24 to plan for the conference. Dorman B. Eaton and Mrs. Richard H. Stewart were named the two delegates of the church to the conference. After the planning committee had been appointed, Mr. Rhoades referred in appropriate terms to the recent death of William, M. Prichard, long a trustee of the church, once its treasurer, "and always one of its most earnest friends and supporters." He said that the society had suffered a serious loss in his death.(9)

At the trustees meeting held on January 10, 1898, a "Minute" was added to Mr. Rhoades words about Mr. Prichard.

A lawyer, Prichard had been treasurer of All Souls from 1858 to 1873, serving on the board of trustees continuously from 1856 to the day of his death. As the minute stated, "hardly any other voice has been heard so often and so effectively in its councils."

A man of singular force of character, clear of insight, sound of judgment, direct and convincing in argument, he has left an impress on the history of the church, and we his associates, cannot pay too high a tribute to his abilities and helpfulness.(10)

The New Minister

Just who was this man, Thomas Roberts Slicer, who at the end of a long search finally was approved unanimously by the congregation of All Souls to lead the church into the twentieth century?

Thomas Roberts Slicer was born in Washington, D.C., on April 16, 1847, the son of Henry and Elizabeth Coleman (Roberts) Slicer. His father was of Scotch descent, and was a prominent minister in the Methodist Episcopal Church. For eight years he was the chaplain of the United States Senate, and knew Abraham Lincoln long before he was elected the sixteenth President of the United States. Thomas was educated in the public schools of Baltimore, and he attended Baltimore City College. He began preaching as a Methodist before he was twenty-one. He was ordained a deacon in 1869 and an elder in 1871. He became famous as a circuit rider on a Maryland circuit of small Methodist churches. He very early received an honorary M. A. from Dickinson College. He then transferred to the Colorado Conference of the Methodist Church, and was pastor at Denver in 1871 and Georgetown in 1872. In 1872 He married Adeline E. Herbert, daughter of Theodore C. Herbert of the United States Navy.

While still quite young he became an associate of the famous Dr. Henry Ward Beecher at Beecher's famous Congregational church in Brooklyn, New York. But Congregationalism was only a halfway station towards where his theological thinking was lead ing him. Even Beecher's rather liberal Congregationalism did not suit him. After several years he felt impelled by changes in his theological views to sever his Methodist connections and to unite with the Unitarians. He served effectively in the First Church in Providence, Rhode Island, from 1881 until 1890. He was then called to Buffalo, New York, where he was the minister from 1890 until in 1897, and, then accepted the call to All Souls Church in New York City. He served at All Souls until his death on May 29, 1916.

Rev. Thomas Slicer appealed to the New York Unitarians partly because he was so effective in many areas of the ministry. He had made a reputation, first of all, as an outstanding preacher. He had the ability of speaking extemporaneously, of expressing his ideas cogently, consecutively, and in a manner that held the close attention of his listeners. Although Bellows was a great man, he was not always a great preacher. His successor at All Souls, Theodore Chickering Williams, although a young man of great promise, grew discouraged, and let his sermon preparation slip badly during the last few years of his ministry. The congregation of All Souls was ready for a powerful preacher. Many of Mr. Slicer's sermons were taken down as delivered by a stenographer, and then printed in a series of books.

His most successful preaching was done in his own pulpit, but he was in great demand in Unitarian churches around the country. While Dr. Slicer was at All Souls he published four volumes of his sermons, *The Great Affirmations of Religion* (1898), *The Foundations of Religion* (1902), *One World At a Time* (1902), and *The Way to Happiness* (1907). These sermons are an attempt to guide those emancipated from the bonds of orthodoxy to a rational religion. One of the fundamental ideas that these sermons stress is that religion is a natural function of the human mind, that religious life consists in developing our better natures to perfection in the individual and in society.

But in addition to being a preacher, Rev. Mr. Slicer also had a poetic bent to his nature, and he was well known for writings in the field of literature. In 1903, he published *Percy Bysse Shelley, an Appreciation.* In 1909 *From Poet to Premier: the Centennial Cycle 1809-1909.* This study offered commentaries on Poe, Lincoln, Holmes, Darwin, Tennyson, and Gladstone, all born in 1809. After his death a selection from his writings, which he had put to gether as an aid to devotion, was published under the title, *Meditations: a Message for All Souls.* So in addition to being a preacher, Slicer was also widely regarded as a literary figure.

A Militant Crusader

Although in religion he believed that the ideal society can be achieved only through the regeneration of the individual, Slicer believed that those who sought this as a personal ideal were also called to combat social evils. To many people, Slicer was known as a militant crusader for civic reform. While in Buffalo, he was in the thick of a fight for clean politics and better municipal institutions. When he came to New York he became a member of the City Club which had been organized to seek good government for the city. He served on the board of trustees of this club. He prepared the charges against District Attorney Asa Bird Gardiner in 1900. Governor Theodore Roosevelt dismissed the charges, but a year later he dismissed Gardiner.

Slicer also carried on a private warfare against gambling institutions which brought him much publicity. He was chairman of the National Commission on Prison Labor. He worked in the councils of the Immigration League, and he was a trustee of the People's Institute. All of these exertions eventually broke down his health, and during the last few years of his life he was ill, and comparatively inactive during the last three or four years of his life.(11)

Influential Parishioners

The first annual meeting of the church after Mr. Slicer became the minister was held on Tuesday evening, January 11, 1898. Frederick F. Forster was elected to fill the unexpired term of Mr. Prichard. For three year terms Richard H. Ewart, J. Lawrence McKeever, and Dorman B. Eaton were elected. It was moved that the trustees be requested to prepare a tablet of either marble or bronze to be erected in the church in memory of the services of William B. Prichard. Mr. Rhoades and Mr. Ewart were requested to prepare a memorial in the records of the society for the services of S. Sidney Smith who had refused to be re-nominated as a trustee. The trustees were also commended for how they "conducted the affairs of the church including the negotiations that resulted in securing for the Society its new Pastor."(12)

Later the trustees entered in the Minute Book a resolution about S. Sidney Smith who had served for fourteen years as a trustee and for thirteen years as the secretary of the board. "Earnest and true in all things, he has ever given his best effort to sustain our church and uphold its dignity in the community in which it is placed."(13)

On January 30, 1898, a special service was held on the occasion of the sixteenth anniversary of the death of Dr. Henry Whitney Bellows. A hymn by Theodore Chickering Williams, "When Thy Heart With Joy O'erflowing," and a hymn that had been written by Henry

Bellows in 1858 for the successful laying of the first Trans-Atlantic Cable, were used. Henry Bellows' son, Rev. Russell N. Bellows, spoke on "The Evolution of a Unitarian Church." That fall the tablet in memory of the services of Mr. Prichard was unveiled. John Harsen Rhoades and Dorman B. Eaton made speeches on this occasion praising William Prichard both for his personal integrity and for what he had done for the church. When the church moved to its present location this plaque was reinstalled on the rear wall of the sanctuary.

On December 23, 1899, Dorman Bridgman Eaton died in his 76th year. He had been not only a prominent lawyer in New York City, but had made a name for himself nationally. Eaton married Annie S. Foster of New York City in 1856, and was admitted to the New York bar. He made rapid progress in the work of the law. One legal controversy grew so bitter that Eaton was set upon and severely injured. Who had done this was never discovered.

He soon became one of the earliest advocates for civil-service reform. It is easy to see why Thomas Slicer appealed to him. William Bennett Munro said of Eaton; "He is entitled to share with George W. Curtis and Carl Schurz the honor of having gained for the merit system its first real recognition in the national administration."(14) From 1870 when he gave up his law practice until his death, he was a courageous and persistent fighter for two causes, the abolition of the spoils system and the reform of city government.

In 1873 President Grant appointed him chairman of the national Civil Service Commission succeeding George W. Curtis who had resigned. Then the Congress cut off the appropriations, and the next President, Rutherford B. Hayes invited Eaton to make a study of the civil-service in Great Britain. He visited Europe and published a well-known book, *The Civil Service in Great Britain: A History of Abuses and Reforms and Their Bearing Upon American Politics.* This book proved of great value in the movement for civil service reform in America. He drafted the bill which became the Pendleton Act of 1883, which remains the basis of the federal civil-service system to the present day. President Arthur then placed Eaton at the head of the Civil Service Commission, and President Cleveland reappointed him in 1885. When he returned to New York City he threw himself into a movement for the reform of the municipal government. He embodied his ideas in another book, *The Government of Municipalities,* which came from the press a few months before his death in 1899. A small volume *Dorman B. Eaton, 1823-1899* was published in 1900. His will provided for two professorships; the "Eaton Professorship of the Science of Government" at Harvard, and the "Eaton Professorship of Municipal Science" at Columbia, both of which have had distinguished occupants. He was typical of the influential people sitting in the All Souls congregation.

A Popular Preacher

Thomas Slicer soon became very popular as a preacher in New York City. George R. Bishop says in a letter written much later in the church archives; "Mr. Slicer was installed, and soon attendance largely grew so that it became the most numerous All Souls had been favored with since the time of Dr. Bellows. His single printed sermons were in great demand, and of the single ones and series the Post Office Mission of the Church circulated tens of thousands of copies."(15)

Samuel Eliot described him as:

a virile preacher, a loyal friend, a citizen identified with many civic and political reforms. Because of his humor, his never-failing supply of pertinent anecdotes and his gift of penetrating speech, he was much in demand as a spokesman at all sorts of civic occasions, and he was constantly in battle against social and industrial wrongdoing. He thoroughly enjoyed stirring up the decorous dullness of an audience, rousing quiescent imaginations, putting some yeast into the solid cake of custom, lifting people out of the ruts of habit. A certain sinewy and sturdy manliness characterized all that he did and said. He made goodness exciting and religion the most interesting thing in the world. He had, too, a way of puncturing shams and bubbles that made some people a bit afraid of him.(16)

It was said that once he began to speak, though previous speakers might have left the audience tired and perhaps some of them asleep, they all became alert, and gave him undivided atten tion when he spoke. The congregation of All Souls carne from a wide geographical field, Brooklyn, Montclair, Yonkers and many other cities outside of Manhattan, and when he died a great number of people attended his funeral at All Souls.

Thomas Slicer was also known as a very accomplished presiding officer and a parliamentarian. He presided over small bodies like the State Conference Board, but he also presided over large assemblies such as the People's Institute, whose meetings filled the large hall of Cooper Union. He was much devoted to the People's Institute, and it was in work such as this that may have contributed to his final prostration.

Routine Meetings

At the Annual Meeting held on January 10, 1899, George F. Baker, Daniel A. Davis, and Frederick Forster were elected as trustees. In January the trustees evidently for the first time invited Mr. Slicer to attend one of their meetings. His name is mentioned in the minutes, and he is also recorded to have made a motion at a special meeting of the congregation on May 21. Usually the minister did not attend such meetings. This shows that Mr. Slicer was held in high esteem by the trustees and the members.(17) Franklin A. Wilcox was appointed to fill the unexpired term of Mr. Eaton. In December Horace J. Hayden, a member of the board of trustees, also died. He had been a trustee for 10 years.(18) At the annual meeting held in the church in January 15, 1901, new three-year term trustees were Lawrence McKeever, Charles H. Strong, and Franklin A. Wilcox. Jed Frye was nominated to fill the vacancy caused by the death of Horace J. Hayden. In 1902 at the annual meeting, George F. Baker, Daniel A. Davis, and Frederick P. Forster were elected trustees. The board of trustees was something of a self-perpetuating group. When someone died a new trustee was appointed, but usually the board remained constant. George F. Baker, for example, was a trustee for fifty years.

Actually, during this period the church must have been functioning very well. There is a kind of rule of inverse proportion when applied to a church which states that the more correspondence the poorer shape the church was in. When very little happened at the annual meetings and the meetings of the board of trustees it can be fairly well ascertained that things must be going well.

The Fiftieth Anniversary of "The Beefsteak Church"

The annual meeting in 1905 was thoroughly routine. The trustees meetings were almost routine. But, the fiftieth anniversary of the building of the 1855 edifice was corning at the end of December, and the board asked Mr. Slicer to be a committee of one to make arrangements for a service of commemoration. Thomas Slicer made arrangements for a Fiftieth Anniversary Service on December 31, 1905. An address which was given by Dr. Robert Collyer, minister emeritus of the Church of the Messiah in New York City, is in the All Souls Archives. It is dated on the day of the anniversary. Although there is no attribution, from internal evidence we can be certain that this is the address of Robert Collyer, written in a large readable hand.

Collyer largely reminisced about Dr. Henry Bellows. He recalled that Bellows had told him "that in the forty years of his ministry in this church, no clergyman in the orthodox churches had ever suggested an exchange of pulpits."(19)

Dr. Collyer remembered the first time he had met Henry Bellows at a meeting of the Western Conference.

"I was then about four years old counting from the time I was a stranger and you Unitarians took me in. Dr. Bellows gave me a warm welcome, and all the work to do my heart could desire. He gave me then and there the right hand of fellowship that was never withdrawn, but stayed strong to the evening when we clasped hands for the last time."(20)

"It was about this time also that the Sanitary Commission was born of which he was not alone the head but the heart, to which the great heart of the nation answered beat for beat."(21) He related the cold-shoulder that Bellows received from the Commander of the Army who resented his intrusion. He told how after Bull Run Bellows had invited him to Washington, and his church in Chicago gave him three month's leave of absence and Collyer took four months. He was then sent to Missouri to look after the sick soldiers in the wake of Freemont's army. "He (Bellows) came west to Chicago to a great Fair, and spoke to some thousands of our people. Then when our great new church was finished in 1869 he (came) out to preach the sermon at the Dedication."(22)

Collyer concluded his reminiscences by making this statement;

"Three men stand alone and apart to me in the great war for the Union and all it meant then and means still; President Lincoln, General Grant, and the minister of this church. The great statesman, the great soldier, and the head of the Sanitary Commission, the grandest agency for help and healing against the awful woes of war the world has ever seen."(23)

Debt Reduction

Over the years a standing debt had been accumulated, and at the meeting of the trustees on January 15, 1906, it was voted that Mr. Strong be appointed to draft a letter to all of the registered members and to all the pew-owners and pew-renters "calling attention to the financial condition of the Society, and urging the members to take sittings or pews in order that the revenues might equal the expenditures."(24) The annual meeting for 1906 was uneventful. But it was reported that the "Deficiency Fund" had reached a total of $25,300, made possible by several large donations; George Baker, $12,500; Mrs. Goodhue, $2,000; Miss Butler, $2,000; Rhoades, Davis, and McKeever $2,000, each, and many other gifts. The money was used to pay off the note at the First National Bank.

Further Honors

In 1914 Brown University conferred on Thomas Roberts Slicer the honorary degree of Doctor of Divinity (D.O.). President Pounce said these words in the commendation:

Doctor of Divinity; Thomas Roberts Slicer, minister to noted churches in Providence and New York; able thinker and forceful speaker; teaching the churches the duty and privilege of civil leadership and the larger meaning of the Kingdom of God.(25)

In regard to Dr. Slicer's preaching abilities George R. Bishop had this to say; "Dr. Cornish, who now has succeeded Dr. Eliot as president of the American Unitarian Association, thought we might perhaps term Dr. Slicer the greatest preacher the denomination ever had."(26)

At Hackley School

Rev. Thomas R. Slicer served on the board of Hackley School in Tarrytown, New York, where his predecessor, Mr. Williams, was the headmaster for a few years until he resigned. A letter in the All Souls Archives from George R. Bishop written after Dr. Slicer died in 1916 indicates that there were some hard feelings between Theodore Williams and Thomas Slicer. When Williams re signed, some his friends tried to place most of the blame on Slicer. George Bishop vehemently disagreed, and said that Thomas Slicer had been a Christian gentleman at all times. "I am perfectly satisfied that Mr. Slicer treated Mr. Williams with great kindness, and consideration, and I know that he kept silent under conditions which would have at least justified some display of temper and irritation. (underlining in original.)

When Dr. Slicer died in New York City on May 29, 1916, the trustees of Hackley School honored his memory with the following citation:

Dr. Slicer was associated with the life and work of the School almost from the beginning and served as Secretary of the Board for fifteen years, retiring only when growing infirmities prevented the continuance of his active cooperation. He brought to the councils of the Board sound judgment, broad experience, and profound sympathy with the hopes and purposes of the School. He promoted its interest through his wide acquaintance, by the power of his forceful speech, his pungent wit, and his reputation as a leader in civic and religious affairs.(27)

The Associate Minister at All Souls, Dr. William L. Sullivan, spoke a few memorial words the Sunday after Dr. Slicer died, which were later reprinted in the *The Christian Register.*(27) Most of the congregation, he said, had known Dr. Slicer at the height of his powers, through his many active years for public decency and civic right. Some few, including Dr. Sullivan himself, only became acquainted with Dr. Slicer in the last three years of his physical de cline. Still, they could see the qualities of the man, even in those days of severe and prolonged prostration.

They stood beside him when, in poignant consciousness that his work was done, he bade farewell to his beloved books and saw one of the best private libraries dispersed at public sale. They watched him as upon his already darkened day fell the somber shadow of his wife's sudden death.

Through all those leaden months of waiting for release, they never heard him once complain. He hallowed illness by the courageous dignity with which he accepted it. . . .

We go back to the task which was ours and his, lifted up in faith and enlarged in charity. . . by this memory which our fellow worker has left behind.

William Laurence Sullivan, Fifth Minister of All Souls
(1916-1922)

CHAPTER 3

A Spirit Aflame

The Ministry of William Laurence Sullivan (1916-1922)

Christ, the immortal example and inspiration of souls who would live in time by ideals beyond it.
From *Under Orders* by William Laurence Sullivan.

The church had taken an unusual step in having two ministers during the last three years of Dr. Slicer's pastorate. This was necessitated, of course, by the fact that Dr. Slicer was in very poor health. In most ways he was not able to function as the minister of the church during the last three years of his life. When Dr. Slicer's health began to fail in 1912, the congregation dwindled because of his inability to occupy the pulpit. The board of trustees of All Souls met and decided to call an associate minister to assist Dr. Slicer. The board looked to a man who was considered to be one of the outstanding Unitarians ministers of the time. Rev. Dr. William Laurence Sullivan was the unanimous choice of the trustees, and he accepted the call to be the associate minister of All Souls.(1) It was fortunate indeed that the trustees and the congregation had the foresight to look ahead, and to call an associate minister who could become the pastor when the older man had to give up his duties.

This was almost thwarted because William Sullivan himself had a genuine fright about his health—a lesion on his lung—and wanted to resign from the associate pastorate. This desire on the part of Mr. Sullivan to resign was prompted not in the mood of either William Ware or Theodore Chickering Williams who were unsure of themselves, but by a genuine desire on Sullivan's part, if he was to endure a lengthy illness, to free the church to look for another associate minister. Sullivan knew that two ministers incapable of performing their functions would only be a double burden on the church.

Fortunately for everyone concerned the lesion was cured, and Sullivan lived a good long life. The trustees' faith in not letting him leave was vindicated, and his own courage carried him through what must have been an illness made difficult by the high hopes that he had of serving the New York church.

A Roman Catholic Background

No more unusual preparation could possibly be imagined than the background that Mr. Sullivan brought to All Souls Church. Dr. Slicer had been the first non-Harvard minister, and the first minister not to have a Unitarian background, coming from Methodist origins. Slicer, in fact, was the son of a Methodist preacher. It could hardly be said that William Laurence Sullivan was the son of a Catholic priest. But his background was about as thoroughly Roman Catholic as was possible. When he left his birthright church he was not only a Catholic priest but a Paulist father, the missionary society of the Catholic Church; those most concerned with conversions to the Catholic faith.

William Laurence Sullivan was born in East Braintree, Massachusetts, on November 15, 1872. His parents, like so many of the Irish immigrants of this period, had come to America only three years prior to his birth. As most immigrants had done, they had settled among their own kind; for Boston and its suburbs, along with New York City, were becoming the largest Irish cities in the entire world. Sullivan's parents had migrated to America from the lovely Irish town of Bandon, County Cork, in the southernmost part of the Emerald Isle not far from where the Irish Sea becomes the Atlantic Ocean.

Like most Catholic children, William Sullivan went to parochial schools, and early he showed a strong inclination to read everything that was put before his eager mind. It is said that by the age of five he had completed The Lives of the Saints. It was after reading this Catholic devotional book that he was filled with so much religious fervor that he decided to add a middle name to his own, and he chose the name Laurence after the Christian martyr Laurence. This martyr whose Latin name was Laurentius (hence the unusual spelling of Laurence) was a deacon of Pope Sixtus II, and according to tradition he was burned alive on an iron grid in the third century.

William Sullivan grew in body and mind, went through high school in Quincy, Massachusetts; and then, like most men headed for the priesthood in those days in the neighborhood of Boston, he went on to study at Boston College. These were years of expanding intellectual horizons for him, and very quickly William Sullivan was noted not only for the seriousness with which he pursued he studies, but the originality and brilliance of his mind. It was predicted by his teachers that he would become one of the leaders of the Roman Catholic Church. In 1896 he received the degree of Bachelor of Philosophy (Ph.B) from Boston College. He had distinguished himself in his studies, especially in English and the Classics, and in his second year had won the coveted Fulton medal for excellence in public debate.

Life As a Priest

Sullivan continued his studies at Catholic University in Washington, D.C. There is a story about the ceremony of tonsure when he took his vows to become a Catholic priest. This ceremony essentially consists in the symbolic cutting of a strand of hair from the head of the candidate for the priesthood. At the time of Sullivan's tonsure the ceremony was to be performed by a most distinguished abbot who was almost totally blind. When Sullivan's turn came he stepped up forward and reverently knelt before the almost sightless abbot. The whole audience gasped almost in unison for suddenly all present became aware that the young man was completely bald, and that the abbot was going to have trouble trying to find a lock of hair. The chapel shook with suppressed laughter as the abbot fumbled frantically, scissors in hand, for the strand of hair that simply was not there.

This period of Sullivan's life was one of continual unfolding. But there were also the inevitable doubts of a man of intellectual talents who began to question some of the premises of the authoritarian system of the Roman Catholic Church. Seminary was the place where these doubts were supposed to be resolved, so Sullivan worked on the difficult intellectual problems which were faced by almost all of his fellow seminarians. Eventually, Sullivan and most of his classmates emerged from their doubt with a strong faith in the authority of the Church. In 1899 Sullivan won the degree of Bachelor of Sacred Theology (S.T.B.) from Catholic University. He spent another year there and earned the further degree of Doctor of Sacred Literature (S.T.L.) from the same institution. Obviously he was destined for some kind of teaching or intellectual position within the Church.

He was ordained into the priesthood in 1899, and he became a member of the Paulist Fathers. This is an American society of the Roman Catholic Church officially named "The Society of Missionary Priests of Saint Paul the Apostle." It was founded in 1858 by Isaac Hecker who felt that there was a place for a missionary order of priests in America who would work for conversions to the Roman Church in ways appropriate to the American scene. The community has remained very small, and besides preaching, its activities today are specialized in such areas as radio and television programs and publishing. The headquarters of the order is in the Church of St. Paul the Apostle in New York City on Fifty Ninth Street just below where Lincoln Center is now located.

For the next ten years William Sullivan spent his time in the profession of teaching for which he seems to be destined and for which he had been trained. He was Professor of Sacred Scripture and Theology at St. Thomas College of Catholic University in Washington, D. C. He was an exceptionally gifted teacher with a thorough knowledge of several languages. In his lectures he would sometimes translate on sight passages from books in German, Italian, French, Hebrew, Latin, or Greek.

He has told of an experience which he once had with another young professor at Catholic University. They had both forgotten on St. Blaise's Day to have their throats blessed at an appropriate ceremony. Since the custom of the day necessitated such a blessing, they decided to bless each other's throats. Then if someone asked them, they could truthfully say that their throats had been blessed. The story, as Dr. Sullivan later told it, was that when they met the next day the fellow priest whose throat Sullivan had blessed had been stricken with laryngitis, and he whispered as best he could into Sullivan's ear: "Heretic!"(2)

Downfall of the "Modernist Movement"

While he was a professor at St. Thomas College, Sullivan became deeply immersed in what was called the Modernist Movement which was gaining strength among the Catholic clergy in both Europe and America. He had high hopes, along with many other young priests, of being part of a movement that would bring the Roman Church abreast of changes in the modern world. But in 1907, the then Pope, Pius X, destroyed all hopes of this possibility with the publication of an encyclical on Papal Infallibility. This set young Sullivan's mind into a topsy-turvy questioning period for two years. To even think of leaving the authoritarian and disciplined priesthood of the Roman Catholic Church was a shattering intellectual and emotional experience. But Sullivan bravely faced all of the possibilities.

Pope Pius X, between the years 1906 and 1914, replaced the few liberals in the Roman hierarchy with reactionaries. In 1907 his Biblical Commission ruled that all Catholics must believe that Moses wrote all of the Pentateuch, that chapters 40-66 of Isaiah were written by one person, that the first woman was formed from Adam's rib, and that all four Gospels were written by those whose names they bear. This decree and others shook the scholarly Catholic world. Then in July 1907, Pope Pius X wrote "Lamentabili" which attacked "Modernism" in all of its aspects. It is not necessary to list these propositions of modernism, but suffice it to say that these propositions would stand today as an expression of what most scholars, including Roman Catholic scholars, believe. This was a sad attempt to stamp out all progress as though it were a heretical sect.

It was not just Dr. Sullivan who was awe-struck that an infallible Pope could speak in this way. The regime was sadly lacking in its understanding and treatment of its intellectuals. The Rev. George Tyrrell was one of these Roman Catholic priests who was forced to recant his beliefs. He was one of the intellectually elite of the Jesuits. He wrote books under various pseudonyms. But he was found out, and was forbidden to celebrate mass. He stayed within the Church, hoping for a kind word that never came. On his deathbed he would not recant. He was absolved of his sins, but refused a requiem mass, and denied burial in a Catholic cemetery.

The Popes were simply refusing to face up to the modern world. Benedict XV and Pius XI did little but continue the trend. Pius XII was an intellectual, but the impression that he gave was that he had the solution to every problem. Catholicism was falling further and further behind the findings of science and the aspirations of modern people.

Resolving His Doubts

At about the same time that Pope Pius X issued his encyclical, William Sullivan became interested in the writings of James Martineau, an English Unitarian minister who lived from 1805-1900, and who preached and wrote books at Liverpool. It will be remembered that it was his sister, Harriet Martineau (1802-1876), an authority on economics and a bitter anti-slavery advocate, who had accompanied Dr. Theodore Pollen on a trip to the Mid-west. Sullivan found James Martineau's rather conservative Unitarian ideas much to his liking, and he made some assignments to his students to read Martineau's books. This aroused some suspicion among his colleagues about what was going on in his mind, and the books were put on the banned list in the college library. When Sullivan had finally resolved his own doubts, he made little secret of his heretical ideas among his friends. He was not joined by throngs of appreciative fellow priests as he might have been after the Second Vatican Council. Instead, he found himself under suspicion, and his former friends often turned their backs on him, at least in public.

The college authorities, having been upset by the assignment of reading in the Martineau books, and his generally known doubts about Papal infallibility, sent William Sullivan to a Catholic Mission in Austin, Texas, so that he might in penitent reflection rid himself of all taints of his heresies. But the problem became worse, for while Sullivan meditated upon the truth of what Martineau had written, the heretical Unitarian ideas became more rather than less real to him. He began to feel that what was branded as heresy was more nearly the truth. So he left the mission in 1909, and he asked to be liberated from the vows of his priesthood. These years were filled with great loneliness and self doubt. He had no teaching positions open to him, certainly not in Catholic schools, and most Protestant seminaries were equally suspicious of his Unitarian ideas. The only employment that he could find was the occasional writing of an article for a newspaper or magazine.

Becoming a Unitarian

In 1910 he moved to Cleveland, Ohio, to live with a former pupil that winter he became a member of the First Unitarian Society of Cleveland which was under the leadership of Reverend Minot Simons, who was eventually to be Sullivan's successor at All Souls Church in New York City. Minot Simons wrote; "It was one of the happiest moments of my life when I extended him the Right Hand of Fellowship in our Unitarian Communion of Free Churches."(3) Charles H. Strong, a prominent member of All Souls and the founder of the national Unitarian Laymen's League, said also about this occasion; "William Laurence Sullivan, the priest in an other faith and order, came from the confessional and the cloister and the creeds into a religious communion, perhaps the most unconventional and freest of all."(4)

Sullivan's stay in Cleveland was brief, for he accepted an invitation to teach History and English in the Ethical Culture School in New York City during the years 1911-1912. He stayed here in 1912, and then he accepted the pulpit of a struggling Unitarian Church in Schenectady, New York. It was in the following year that the trustees of All Souls approached him to be come the associate minister of All Souls Church in New York City. He accepted the call on the condition that for at least a year he could help the Schenectady church in its struggle to exist and to find a successor. But this double duty was too much for him, and overwork necessitated his leave of absence for several months in 1915. Undoubtedly, some of the people who were members at All Souls Church had become acquainted with Mr. Sullivan while he was teaching at the Ethical Culture School in New York City. It is highly probable that he attended church at All Souls for it is somewhat doubtful if his loyalty and sympathies would have been with the young radical and pacifist minister, John Haynes Holmes, who was now the minister of the Church of the Messiah.

Perhaps he even preached occasionally at All Souls for Dr. Slicer was ailing, although the records are incomplete, and there is no evidence for such preaching engagements. Dr. Slicer was not only ill, but he was away from the city for long periods of time trying to recover his health, and the church was constantly in need of supplies for the pulpit. A year later when they were looking for an associate minister the name of Sullivan appeared to be well known to the trustees, and they did not do any candidating with other ministers. This implies that they knew William Sullivan rather well. After serving for three years as the associate minister he succeeded to the ministry of All Souls on the death of Dr. Slicer late in May 1916.

In 1916, Mr. Sullivan went to the Pacific Coast for a series of preaching engagements, and preached over forty sermons during a single month. That he was an excellent lecturer is attested by the fact that he received the signal honor of being asked to give the Dudleian Lecture at Harvard University in 1917.

As was the case with Theodore Williams, the ministry of William Laurence Sullivan was enhanced by the qualities that his wife possessed in relationship to the people of All Souls. Contrary to the experience of many priests who have left the Church in order to get married, William Sullivan did not meet his future wife, Estelle Throckmorton of Washington, D. C., daughter of Hugh William and Rebecca (Upton) Throckmorton of Virginia, until he had spent a year teaching at the Ethical Culture School in New York City. After their marriage she was constantly at his side as a helper. It was she who began the church calendar, although we have no copies that I can discover. She served the dinner, or made plans for its serving, at the annual meeting in 1919. She also directed the Sunday School. They lived at 419 West 119th Street which was quite a distance from the church. As a result, William Sullivan spent a great deal of his time in his study at his residence rather than at the church.

In December, 1916, Dr. Sullivan began a monthly publication title "Faith and Freedom," which was termed "A monthly messenger from All Souls Unitarian Church, Fourth Avenue and Twentieth Street, New York; a church of the Free Spirit, holding to all that is eternal in religion, character, aspiration, worships—but refusing to bind itself or its members to the statements of ecclesiastical creeds."(5) Sullivan believed that sermons were not enough. "If each church is to make itself a sort of university of the spirit, it must give to its words the wings of the printed page. In no other way can it reach, or have any fair chance of reaching the crowd which will not yet listen, but may still read."(6)

One of the reasons that Sullivan gave for his new venture was that he had heard two ministers of his acquaintance say that "the war put an end to any faith they might have had in a Spirit transcending our human sphere."(7) But Sullivan believed that the opposite was true, that the war had actually produced a revival of religion in the belligerent countries. He knew that men in anguish turn to the only faith they know. He also began to publish his sermon topics, hoping, of course, to lure a few more curious worshippers to All Souls. He also told his readers that articles which appeared in "Faith and Freedom" were the work of the minister of the church, unless otherwise stated.

The annual meeting of the congregation was held early in January, 1917, and as Mr. Sullivan was detained in Cambridge by some denominational business, he wrote out his remarks to the congregation. He wrote that he wanted to mention three items. The first was that there was to be a minute of silence after the prayer in the Sunday morning service. He had tried this, and there had been strong objections. He would abide by the vote of the congregation after there had been some experiments. He didn't believe the minute of silence would hurt anyone. He also felt that the time was not too early to appoint a committee to plan for the 100th anniversary of the founding of the Church which would take place in November, 1919. He was also concerned that there be some more formal procedure about greeting people when they came to church. He also mentioned the purpose of the new journal "Faith and Freedom" which was still in the experimental stage. He was writing the magazine in its entirety now, but he would welcome contributions.(8)

In 1917 Mr. Sullivan became Doctor Sullivan when Meadville Theological School, the Unitarian seminary in Chicago, awarded him the honorary degree of Doctor of Divinity (D.O.) To this was added a second doctorate late in his life when Temple University in Philadelphia awarded him an honorary Doctor of Laws (LL.D.) in 1934. He was also honored in 1917 by being asked to give the Anniversary Sermon at the Unitarian May Meetings in Boston. He also gave the Dudleian Lecture at Harvard in 1917.

The War and All Souls

By April of 1917, when America entered the European War, Mr. Sullivan was most emphatic about where he stood in the matter of the war. He encouraged his readers to "think straight and to feel straight on the significance of our step for our own history and the world's."(9) He enjoined his readers to be prepared for sacrifices. In the same issue of April 1917, he wrote an article on "Why We Are at War." He claimed that America had not entered the war to vindicate general international law, or because we had taken sides in the original quarrel between belligerent European groups, nor because we had decided that the injuries done to us by Germany were greater, nor because of our touchy sense of honor, nor because our vessels have been sunk, nor because American lives have been destroyed in the submarine blockade.

Then he listed two reasons why America was at war; that Germany had announced they will take American lives not casually but systematically, and to prevent the political and military leaders of a great state from killing innocent persons. These copies of "Faith and Freedom" are very valuable in showing the mindset of one of our great American ministers during the First World War. The All Souls copies of "Faith and Freedom" end with the February-March issue of 1919. Here is a place for a much more detailed study as to how a metropolitan church in New York City, or at least its minister, felt about the issues of the war. Whereas Dr. Sullivan spoke a great deal about the war in "Faith and Freedom," the only indication in the church records that the United States had been drawn into the great European War in April of 1917 is that the trustees authorized Mr. Sullivan to prepare and send a letter to President Woodrow Wilson at the outbreak of the war. The United States had broken off diplomatic relations with Germany in February, 1917, and declared war on April 6, 1917. The All Souls' trustees authorized this letter on April 3 while the United States Senate was still debating the issue of whether the United States would declare war on Germany. The trustees left the matter completely in Mr. Sullivan's hands.

The language of this document is indicative of the enthusiasm for the war felt at least by the minister and trustees of
All Souls Church.

*"Mr. Sullivan having suggested that the church be true to
its traditions and send its declaration of approval to Pres.
Wilson, it was voted unanimously that Mr. Sullivan be authorized, in the name of the church, to draft and send to
Pres. Wilson such a declaration as he may deem fit—such
declaration to be signed at his discretion either by Mr. Sullivan or add to his name, the names of the trustees."*

Mr. Sullivan prepared such a letter. He declared that the church
sends "this declaration of unreserved support." Mentioning the
work of Henry Bellows and the United States Sanitary Commission during the Civil War, Mr. Sullivan continued in the vein of a
professor of moral philosophy;

*War, we believe, is to be judged morally by its motive and
end. To look only on its material and physical aspect is for-
getfulness of motive and end, is to reduce to one scale wars
for liberty and wars for crime, and to regard as on one level
the aggression of tyrants who would wreck the structure of
civilization, and the resistance of patriots in whose graves the
pillars of the temple of freedom rest. . . No war may be called
right or wrong until we know what it aims to do, whether
the end is proportionate to so grave a means. Judged by this
standard of straight-sighted ethics, the war now begun by the
United States is just. For its purpose is to prevent a relatively
small body of political and military leaders, who demand the
world's recognition of their right to kill innocent persons on
the high seas, from winning their way now, and perhaps in the
event of their victory, from forcing this fateful principle into
the body of international precedents. . . . The patriot's and
the Christian's duty are here one and the same. A righteous
end is to be won and must be won; and if by force, it is not the*

first time in the world's history or in our own that men who
hate war have had to turn to that last resource of Right.(10)

Mr. Sullivan then pledged his own efforts and those of his congregation behind the war effort.

This declaration of the rightness of war is interesting to us not because it was unusual for its time, but because it was so typical of the way in which the churches of the country responded to the entrance of the United States into the First World War, for which the churches were later strongly criticized. One could have known immediately, whether Mr. Sullivan's name was on the letter or not, that he was its author. The language is so typically his, yet the sentiments must have been those of the great majority of his congregation as they were those of the rest of the country.

A Contrary Stance

On the other hand, at the Church of the Messiah, the daughter Church of All Souls, founded as an offshoot in 1825, an entirely different opinion was expressed by the minister, John Haynes Holmes. Holmes had candidated for this pulpit in November,1906, and was called to be the associate minister in February, 1907. He was a socialist, a pacifist, and opposed the entry of the United States into the first World War. His point of view was at the opposite pole from that of Mr. Sullivan, and although the two men respected each other, the advent of Holmes on the New York Unitarian scene ten years prior to this time had given Unitarianism in New York City a radical aura that was strongly resented by the members of All Souls.

The ancestry of John Haynes Holmes went directly back to the Plymouth of 1620 on his father's side. His mother's Puritan family, Haynes, immigrated to Boston in 1635. Thus Holmes' ancestry was a combination of Pilgrim and Puritan. Marcus Norton Holmes, his father, and Alice Haynes Holmes moved to Philadelphia shortly after their marriage in 1879. On November 29,

1879, their first child was born and named for his grandfather on his mother's side, John Haynes. The family moved back to the vicinity of Boston. At the age of fifteen John entered Malden High School, and his teachers were soon convinced that he ought to go on to college. In Boston that meant Harvard, and there largely on scholarship aid, young Holmes went through Harvard College and then was graduated from the Harvard Divinity School. He won a Phi Beta Kappa key, which he proudly wore, and he knew as early as his sophomore year that he wanted to enter the ministry.

John Haynes Holmes was in large part motivated by the example of Reverend Theodore Parker, Dr. Minot Savage, and the presence in Boston of some great preachers. His grandfather, John Cummings Haynes, had been a member of Parker's original congregation in Boston. Reverend Minot Savage was then the minister of the Church of the Unity in Boston, and young Holmes went to hear Savage often with his grandfather. At the church on Hollis Street, Savage would preach for an hour with not a scrap of paper in front of him. His sermons were taken down stenographically, and then were printed each week. They have been a large influence in my preaching, for my predecessor at The First Unitarian Church in Worcester was Minot Savage's son, Maxwell Savage, and Dr. Savage gave me his copies of his father's printed sermons which filled many volumes. They read quite well even at this time.

When Holmes attended the Harvard Divinity School it was a time of great teachers, men such as Francis Greenwood Peabody, George Foot Moore, Kirsop Lake, and many others. Holmes loved Harvard and all of its traditions. He also taught Sunday School at the First Unitarian Society located in Harvard Square. He worked in the Unitarian Church in Danvers as his student parish. He met his wife, Madeleine Hosmer Baker in Brooklyn, and they were engaged for many years while he finished his schooling. By this time Minot Savage was the Minister of the Church of the Messiah in New York City, and he impressed Holmes again and again when he came to Cambridge to preach. In 1904 John Haynes Holmes both married Miss Baker and took charge of a church in Dorchester.

Very shortly Holmes was under consideration as an associate for the aging Dr. Robert Collyer at the Church of the Messiah in New York City. Minot Savage had suffered a mental and physical breakdown, and Collyer at the age of 83 was filling in after Savage's decline. Holmes came to New York in February, 1907. The Church of the Messiah was a staid old-fashioned New York Church. Holmes says that his choice was "a sheer gamble on the fulfillment of my youthful promise as a public speaker."(11)

When Minot Savage had retired due to his complete break down of health, the congregations which had packed the auditorium each Sunday disappeared as completely as the preacher. When Holmes came, the church had only 160 members on its rolls. John Holmes early offended many of the older members. He claimed that what many of the people wanted was not a church but a private chapel. The Church of the Messiah was a purely conventional institution, but John Haynes Holmes was anything but conventional. When the war came Holmes' paci fistic and socialistic views drove away almost all who would not back his ideas. Some backed him even if they did not agree with him. This was the pastor of the Church of the Messiah whom Mr. Sullivan called "colleague." But the two of them were in many ways as different as night and day.

A Fire and Its Aftermath

The Armistice that marked the end of the First World War came on November 11, 1918, and peace returned, or some semblance of it. But tragedy almost immediately hit the congregation of the Church of the Messiah. On the afternoon and evening of September 11, 1919, the Church of the Messiah burned to the ground. John Holmes said that those who saw the fire called it "a vast caldron of heat and horror."(12) Holmes tells of an all-night trip on the railroad from his Maine summer home:

The streets were quiet and the air cool, as I walked eight blocks south (from Grand Central Station) to my ruined church. I looked first at the foundations of the church, shaken and burned, and laden with wreckage. Then my eyes moved upward-the lectern and pulpit gone, or badly damaged, the great new organ an empty shell, the majestic balconies crushed and burned, like hulks beaten to pieces on a rocky shore. Then, far aloft, the crossbeams of the roof woven and interwoven like strands of a spider's web. Here the wreckage was almost complete.(13)

That first Sunday after the fire the officers of All Souls had invited the congregation of the Church of the Messiah to meet in their edifice. Had the discordant conflicts over patriotism and socialism been forgotten? Well, they had for one Sunday at least.

But what happened within the official family of All Souls was not so stirring nor so emotional. No two churches could have been more polarized than the ministers and the congregations of the two Unitarian Churches in New York City.

The congregation of All Souls in typically patriotic mood that pervaded the country during the war had sent a pledge of support to President Wilson. If ever a church had entered into politics it was All Souls in sending this resolution.

But the Church of the Messiah under the leadership of John Haynes Holmes was on exactly the opposite side, for Holmes was a pacifist. He opposed the war. He declared himself a conscientious objector to the war. Those in the congregation who could not stomach his point of view left, and a few of them may have come to All Souls. This extreme difference in point of view about the war created a feeling of separation between the congregations that still persisted when I became the minister of All Souls in 1955. During my ministry Dr. Donald Harrington and I exchanged pulpits, probably the first exchange since the First World War. But when I first suggested the exchange the board of All Souls was not in favor, although later the mood changed to one of cooperation. But that was not until the late nineteen sixties.

The board of trustees of All Souls met on September 23,

almost two weeks after the destruction of the Church of the Messiah. The board even invited Dr. Sullivan to be present. Mr. Strong, the president of the board, stated that they were gathered to resolve a controversy about the use of their building by the Church of the Messiah, and added pointedly "of which the Reverend John Haynes Holmes is the minister."(14)

Mr. Strong further stated that he had received a telegram from the president of the American Unitarian Association, Dr. Samuel A. Eliot, urging All Souls to extend its hospitality to the "homeless church." Mr. Strong had not even known about the fire as he was away on vacation in Connecticut. But when notified, he telegraphed the sexton of the church to get into immediate communication with Mr. Sullivan, and if the minister did not disapprove, to offer Mr. Holmes the hospitality of the church. This was done, and William Sullivan indicated that he had intended to offer this hospitality even before Mr. Strong's message had reached him. Dr. Sullivan had also stated; "I can see no way out except to offer them All Souls for evening services once our own services begin."(15)

The trustees of the Community Church, which during the year 1919 had changed its name from the Church of the Messiah to the Community Church of New York City, were pleased to receive the offer to hold their services on the morning of September 28th, All Souls' services not yet having commenced for the fall season. Learning that Mr. Kissel, a member of the standing com mittee, disapproved of such use of the church, Mr. Strong had endeavored to call a meeting of the standing committee, but a quorum could not attend.

At the trustees' meeting on September 23rd, Mr. Strong asked for ratification of his actions. Each trustee present and Dr. Sullivan expressed his views. "Mr. Sullivan also stated that Mr. Holmes was to hold only one service in All Souls Church, and that the sermon was to be nearly in the nature of a conference about what the Community Church should do in view of the fire."(16)

This was getting at the gist of the controversy, for what several of the trustees obviously feared was that John Haynes

Holmes would express some of his unacceptable political views
from the pulpit of All Souls. George F. Baker made a motion that
the action of Mr. Strong be approved. Baker, Nutting, Fraser, and
Delano voted in favor, and Mr. Hemphill, the former president
of the board, voted in the negative. It was to be presumed that
Mr. Kissel if he had also been present, would also have voted in
the negative.

"Mr. Hemphill thereupon presented his resignation as a member of the Board of Trustees and as a member of the congregation.
On motion; his resignation was laid on the table." Feelings were
obviously running very high on the matter. Nothing was done
about Mr. Hemphill's resignation at a further meeting of the board
on October 29 although he was present. At the next meeting on
December 21, Mr. Strong made the suggestion that Mr. Hemphill's resignation be taken up for discussion, and that "Mr. Hemphill wished it withdrawn." It was decided by unanimous vote that
this resignation not be accepted."(17)

Alexander Hemphill, around whom this incident revolved,
was born in Philadelphia in 1856, and died in New York City a
year after this incident, on December 20, 1920. He was at first
connected with the Pennsylvania Railroad, and then moving to
New York City about 1903, he became one of the financial leaders of the city. During the war he was the treasurer of the Belgian
Relief Committee. For many years he and his family occupied a
pew in the church. He was first elected to the board of trustees in
1908, served as president during the war years from 1915-1919.
He then became the church treasurer for a year until his death. It
is no wonder that in 1919 his sentiments were not those of John
Haynes Holmes, and that he objected so strongly that his beloved
church be used by someone whose sentiments about the recent
war were exactly the opposite of his own.

Obviously the trustees, and probably the congregation, were
deeply split on this matter. Fortunately, it was not necessary to
debate the matter in full at a congregational meeting as it would
have been embarrassing to the Community Church as well as to
All Souls. The Community Church found a hall where they could

worship on Sunday mornings rather than in the evenings at All Souls, and the matter was resolved without further discussion. Mr. Hemphill was so emotionally overcome as to resign both from the board and the church, but four months later he realized that what he had done was hasty, and there was no longer any issue, so there was peace in the All Souls family. I have told this story in full because it has scarcely been aired before, and it is indicative of the strong feelings that existed between the two sister churches over the issues of the First World War and pacifism. Not that the members of All Souls were militarists, but we realize now from our vantage point many years later that pacifism is now a very different issue. But in the early twentieth century it was placed in the same class as socialism and bolshevism as being communistic and unthinkable.

The Centennial Year

Nineteen nineteen was also the hundredth anniversary of the founding of All Souls Church. It was decided that the project of the centennial year would be the raising of a $100,000 fund to pay off the long-standing debt on the church, and to start an endowment fund. The church had been built with enthusiasm in 1855, but the over-enthusiasm of the architect, Jacob Wrey Mould, had created an edifice with the bell tower never completed, some serious space problems, and a large debt.

A celebration was held on November 15th and 16th in honor of the centennial year, and in celebration of the completion of the raising of the $100,000 Centennial Fund. Dr. Charles W. Eliot, former president of Harvard, and a brother-in-law of Henry Bellows, president Amos Lawrence Lowell of Harvard, and former President and now Chief Justice Howard Taft, a Unitarian, were among the speakers. Dr. Eliot spoke of the progress of religion from terror to love, from servitude to freedom, and laid emphasis upon the immortal service given to these forward thrusts by the Unitarian movement. Chief Justice Howard Taft spoke about his own devotion to the Unitarian religion, and dwelt upon the grandeur of religion for the private soul and the church's importance in society. Dr. Sullivan spoke, as did Dr. John Lathrop of the Brooklyn church. Both the Church of the Savior in Brooklyn and the church in Harlem closed their doors to join in the celebration. A pamphlet published during the centennial year was the closest thing to a written history of the church until I began to write the history of All Souls beginning before the 150th celebration in 1969. It has now lengthened into three volumes.

A Need for Symbolism

The annual meeting of 1920 proved to be a most interesting one indeed, for the All Souls branch of the Layman's League un der the able leadership of Charles H. Strong, made a report in which some suggestions for the improvement of the general wel fare of the church were considered. Church attendance was on the decline, and this report stated that other churches "are devoting more and more attention to the development of ecclesiastical at mosphere in their churches."(18) To bring more "ecclesiastical atmosphere" into the basilica that was All Souls, the report suggest ed some practical ideas.

The first of these was to "carry out Dr. Sullivan's often expressed wish to put up a Cross or other evidence of the Divine, back of the pulpit."(19) This eventually was carried out and a cross was put on the communion table in front of the pulpit rather than at the back of the pulpit. We shall see that this has been a continuing bone of contention among the congregation. When the new church was built in 1932, there was no cross until 1940. It continued to be an issue which we shall discuss during my ministry.

Symbolism has long been of concern to churches, especially liberal ones. Dr. Sullivan, with his strong emotional background in Roman Catholicism, in spite of his intellectual break with his former religious beliefs, must have felt keenly the barrenness of a church with little or no symbolism. One can well ask, can you build a copy of a Byzantine cathedral and then keep it barren of symbolism? The answer evidently was that something was needed, and the congregation agreed with Dr. Sullivan that the symbol of the cross would suffice.

In a day when new Unitarian buildings are not built in a traditional architectural pattern there is often no symbolism whatso ever. The cross that was installed in All Souls is often given explanations by persons from other religious backgrounds which is not what is meant by the congregation. Usually this cross is misunderstood because traditional symbolism is read into this simple cross. The congregation also wanted the rather barren east wall of the church to be enlivened with some form of decoration, and suggested that an expert be consulted to look into the possibilities.

On Being Long-Winded

William Sullivan was well known for his "long-windedness." This applied not only to his preaching but particularly to his prayers. Smce he had such an interest in things religious he often mistakenly assumed that others automatically shared his interest. As a mission preacher in the Catholic Church in the order of Saint Paul he was used to giving long sermons. At this annual meeting of the congregation the "longwindedness" surfaced. Some members of the congregation felt that the length of the service should be limited to one hour and a quarter. This was voted down, as was a suggestion that "the voluntary extemporaneous prayer" be shortened.

There was then a cryptic motion that the length of the prayer be limited to five minutes. Prayers in the church today would seem like short-hand notes compared to the flowing cadences of Dr. Sullivan's prayers. But this was not voted on. There was also a discussion about whether the minister should be allowed a fifteen or twenty word prayer at the conclusion of the sermon, and seven persons spoke for and against this idea. It was accepted. When the business meetings of the congregation were so often devoted to practical matters, it is refreshing to find the congregation discussing some of the religious aspects of their worship services.

A Call to a New Duty

At the annual meeting in 1921 held on January 11, it was announced that Alexander Hemphill had died. Also, Warren Delano had died. His daughter, Sara Delano, married Franklin Roosevelt, and they were the parents of Franklin Delano Roosevelt. On January 25 Charles H. Strong resigned as a trustee since his work on the national Laymen's League was taking up so much of his time. During the year also there was correspondence with Minot Simons who was director of the Department of the Ministry at the American Unitarian Association about the possibility for an associate minister at All Souls. Rev. Palfrey Perkins of Weston, Massachusetts, appeared to be interested, although nothing came of it. Mr. Perkins was later the minister of King's Chapel in Boston.

Just one year later, Dr. Sullivan resigned as the minister of All Souls Church. On January 2, 1922, Dr. Sullivan announced to the president of the board of trustees that he had accepted the invitation of the National Layman's League to become their "Missionary Minister." He stated that it had been a most difficult decision to make, for he had become deeply attached to the people of All Souls. He felt, however, that the invitation from the League was a "call to duty" that he could not decline however difficult it might be.

He knew that there would be a gap before the congregation could find a new minister. He agreed not to take up his new duties until a successor had been found. He said that he felt that "more than likely the change will help the church. A new man, a new voice, a new way of doing things, will probably invigorate the work of the congregation, and stimulate all of its activities."(20)

Mr. R. H. Bissel, the president of the board, accepted the resignation, and asked Dr. Sullivan to address the congregation at its forthcoming annual meeting. The congregation responded by asking that his letter of resignation be reconsidered. Dr. Sullivan did reconsider, and found his duty the same as previously. Charles Strong spoke of the services of Mrs. Sullivan to the life of the church. She was a much beloved figure, and the members at the meeting expressed their deep appreciation for her services. A resolution for her was spread upon the minutes.(21) Then a resolution was prepared to honor Dr. Sullivan.

In expressing its appreciation the congregation had much to say; "We feel with him that duty calls him to this great work and that as a single congregation we have no right to stand in the way of such a service."(22) They listed the handicaps under which the church was suffering, but added, "In spite of these handicaps the membership has steadily increased. The interior of the church has been transformed by the shifting of the organ, giving us the great window on the north, and by decorating the somber walls and supplying an adequate and much needed lighting system." (23) These were practical considerations indeed. But then their appreciation moved to a more personal level; "His glowing words have lighted the first of our enthusiasm and made us feel that this church and other Unitarian Churches of America are worth working and sacrificing for. A new hope and a new faith have been born in our hearts and it is here we must look for the secret of any advance which we have made."(24)

A Missionary Minister

Exactly what was this greater mission to which Dr. Sullivan was called by the Layman's League, the national men's organization of the Unitarian denomination? This was a time when Protestantism was on the march, and there were strong feelings that what constituted Unitarian belief should no longer be hid under a bushel, but put on a hill. Dr. Sullivan often during his ministry at All Souls had gone for a week's preaching mission to some community. He would speak every evening, and there would be an intense effort on the part of the local congregation

to get a good attendance with parties and suppers.
It was a kind of religious emphasis week. The Layman's
League emphasized the former Roman Catholic relationship of
Dr. Sullivan. It was not an anti-Catholic mission, but there was
every effort to show that one Catholic priest at least had seen
the Unitarian light. Having been so successful in this, one of All
Souls' own members, Charles H. Strong, who was the national
president of the Layman's League had raised the necessary funds
to make this a continual project so that Dr. Sullivan could devote
all of his energies to this task without the problem of serving a local parish church. And after all, Dr. Sullivan had been trained as a
missionary priest by the Paulist Fathers.

The New Covenant

The annual meeting was adjourned until February 10 in 1922, because in addition to passing resolutions about Dr. and Mrs. Sullivan the congregation was to turn its attention to a very important
matter which has important connotations to everyone who joins
the Unitarian Church of All Souls at the present time. The meeting concerned itself with an amendment to the By-Laws, and for
the first time the present day covenant or Bond of Union appears
in the By-Laws. The old covenant which has been adopted in Dr.
Bellows' time was outmoded.(25) The new covenant suggested
was one that had been adopted over the years by many Unitarian
churches, indicating a new freedom in covenants: "In the freedom
of the truth, and in the spirit of Jesus, we unite for the worship of
God, and the service of man."(26)
    Mr. Strong moved:

*"that the Bond of Union as adopted at this meeting be
written in the membership book after the last of the sig-
natures now entered, and that all persons signing thereafter should thus expressly adopt the Bond of Fellowship; and that, in order that those who have heretofore*

signed might be given an opportunity thus expressed to adopt the Bond of Fellowship, all such persons should be notified by the secretary that unless objection should be received by him in writing within thirty days after such notice, such express adoption of the Bond of Fellowship by each of them should be assumed."

This was a way of adopting a new covenant, and assuring those who had signed under the old covenant that they had an opportunity in freedom of conscience to adopt or reject the new one. The names of several persons who objected to the new covenant are listed in the membership book.(27) Thus All Souls Church was still in the tradition of the New England covenant churches in which the covenant was stated in general terms, and there was no specific interpretation of the individual words of the covenant leaving that to individual belief and conscience.

A Group Ministry?

The selection of a new minister seemed to be a simple matter, but as we shall see it almost split the church, and led four trustees to resign. The search committee heard several candidates, but there was no unanimity. It was at this point that Dr. Sullivan, perhaps getting a little impatient under the long delay and hoping to begin his "missionary ministry," made the suggestion of a group ministry. He made the suggestion (and this plan was later adopted by the Germantown Church where he served) that the church call a regular minister who might preach on the average about once a month. The pulpit was to be filled on most Sundays by the greatest preachers of the time. These preachers need not necessarily be Unitarian ministers but could include ministers of other denominations or members of the faculty of divinity schools whose beliefs were not antithetical to Unitarian beliefs.

Through this collegium, as it was termed, Dr. Sullivan believed that it would be easier to secure a minister, for he need not be a great preacher. The congregation would also have the benefit of hearing pluralistic religious points of view. But there developed a sharp division within the congregation on this matter. It was bantered about all of the year. Four of the trustees—E. Morgan Grinnell, Ralph H. Kissell, William B. Nichols, and Robert Ramsey—became so disgusted with the wavering of the congregation on the group ministry plan that they refused to continue serving as trustees. These four trustees were totally opposed to the plan. There has been some rumblings that Dr. Sullivan was too long-winded in his prayers and his sermons, but he was much beloved, and the main impetus for the resignation of these trustees was specifically the plan for a group ministry.(28)

As a result of these resignations, at the annual meeting in 1923 it was necessary to elect seven persons to fill out a board of nine members. This resulted in the election of the first two woman trustees of the church: Miss Georgina Schuyler and Mrs. John R. McGinley. There was so much concern about the controversy that the congregation asked Dr. Samuel A. Eliot, the president of the American Unitarian Association, the address an adjourned meeting of the congregation on January 22, 1923.

Dr. Eliot, son of president Charles W. Eliot of Harvard University, in his suave way suggested five possibilities to the congregation: 1. Select a minister in the usual way; 2. Request Mr. Sullivan to return; 3. Look for a minister among other denominations of a liberal faith; 4. Consider calling a minister from overseas (a practice long popular among New York City churches); or 5. Resume consideration of having a Board of Preachers. Eventually the congregation gave consideration only to the first option, to select a minister in the usual way. The idea of a collegium had caused too much rumpus to be seriously considered, and calling a minister in the regular way appeared to be the only way out of the dilemma. We shall see how the calling of Dr. Minot Simons came about in the next chapter of our history.

Final Years

Because of his poor health, Dr. Sullivan was only able to spend two years on the Layman's League assignment. It was an exhausting schedule. He toured the United States and lectured al most every evening during those two years. He was promoted as a former priest who had become a Unitarian, and he held count less "conversion" meetings in many American cities which were very effective. He then accepted a call to the Unitarian Church of the Messiah in Saint Louis, Missouri, and remained there for two years. He was then called to Germantown, Pennsylvania, a suburb of Philadelphia, where he spent the remaining six years of his life until he died there on October 5, 1935.

What Manner of Man?

A little known and little used analysis of Dr. Sullivan and his theological break from the Roman Catholic Church is to be found in the pages of a book by John Ratte titled, Three Modernists: Alfred Loisy, George Tyrrell, William L. Sullivan. It is the most thorough study that I have found of his theological ideas, and of his spiritual pilgrimage. The author begins with a rather thorough study of Sullivan's background. Sullivan said of his parents:

> *They reared me sternly, with true affection for me but with no extravagant display of it. . . Their Catholicism had not a bit of sentimentality in it. . . They interpreted their religion as a school of courage and decency.(29)*

The turning point in Sullivan's career Dr. Ratte says, came at the age of fifteen when he decided to enter the religious life. Sullivan was able to balance devotional fervor and theological development. But in seminary he found that; "if anything, his discovery of the irrelevance of seminary apologetics to the world of skepticism and materialism encouraged both his vocation and his conviction that ecclesiology was at the heart of religious studies."(30) Ratte says that "the death of his mother in the spring of 1897 freed Sullivan to make a decision he had long entertained, and he resolved to enter the Paulists."(31) Looking back, Sullivan recalled the joyous fraternity of the Paulists.(32)

But he found the theology in Washington little better than the theology of Boston. He sometimes marveled how some of his teachers could live bodily in the nineteenth century, and in their mental life live in the twelfth, tenth, or fifth centuries. He felt that the professors and the priests had little relevance with the world outside of the seminary.

He became one of the chief critics of modern Protestantism. "As a church, Protestantism had become little more than the code of conduct of a good man's conscience enhanced by the moral authority of a purely human Christ who lived without sin or imperfection."(33) He believed that in America the Catholic Church would go the same way that it had in France unless Catholics worked for the spread of their religion. He also believed that the Church was not facing the questions of science in a confrontation of religious beliefs. He became deeply distressed and disillusioned with the prospects in the Church for the acceptance of modern thought and scientific thought. By the year 1906 Sullivan believed that he was as orthodox in his belief as he had been while in the seminary, but he began to believe that he was fated to take a position with the Modernists. But he also discovered that many of his fellow priests had been troubled by critical questions. There was even talk among some of the professors that the infallibility of the church was outmoded and would have to go. One president of a Catholic theological seminary told Sullivan that "I could no more pray to the Trinity than I could to a triangle."(34)

Writings By A Modernist

But Sullivan was bothered by all of this unbelief, and he thought that some of the priests did not realize the moral implications or their new beliefs, or unbeliefs. He could not conceal his growing anxieties. In 1908 he asked to be transferred to parish work. He first went to Chicago. There he met a priest-professor who told Sullivan that he had simply closed his mind to all doubts. But this interview was hardly designed to answer the perpetual inquiries which filled Sullivan's mind. He soon began to believe that a reform of Catholicism was a hopeless cause. His "Ideal Catholicism" remained a hope, "but as he sketched it in *Letters to His Holiness Pius X, by a Modernist,* and in his novel, *The Priest,* it had nothing to do with Roman Catholicism and was Christian only in the most liberal sense."(35)

In his book to Pius X,. the words "by a Modernist" had been printed in very small type. America was largely ignorant of the Modernist Movement within the Catholic Church. He still believed that if the Catholic Church could have life anywhere, the ideal Catholicism of the future would grow in America. "We know," Sullivan wrote, "what the American spirit is in the political and social order. Translate it into the religious order, and you have Modernism at its best and purest."(36) America had what Catholicism lacked: freedom. He believed that the American doctrine of the separation of church and state was one of the finest products of American civilization. America was an embodiment of the "gospel" of democracy, free personalities should be governed under freedom. He was still struggling with his dilemma, and the autobiographic novel, *The Priest, A Tale of Modernism in New England,* was the result in 1911, and a reprint was needed in 1912 so great was the demand for the book.

In this novel the hero is Father Ambrose Hanlon, who like Sullivan was trained at Brighton and sent to Rome for graduate study. He is given the assignment of establishing a new parish in the town of Axton, a bastion of rural Unitarianism which had recently been invaded by Catholics from Ireland. The Protestants were led in politics by a last Puritan, Squire Wakefield, and in religion by a young Unitarian minister, Josiah Danforth. The two men quickly became friends. They lead each other into realms that they had never studied in their seminaries. There were also problems, however, with Unitarianism, for "Unitarianism," unfortunately, had become so much less rigid in its doctrines and creeds as to threaten to dissolve completely. Ministers of the Liberal Fellowship were to be heard preaching pantheism, or any other sort of ethical paganism.(37) Eventually the bishop cracked down on Father Hanlon, and he was forbidden the reading of Protestant books. But in the minds of both of these ministers of religion the priesthood had been exchanged for prophecy, and the kingdom of Heaven had been transformed into the kingdom of character.

A Unitarian Catholic, a Catholic Unitarian

William Laurence Sullivan chose a more outwardly conventional path than his fictitious priest. In going from the priesthood and the Roman Catholic Church to marriage and the American Unitarian Association, he did what no other Modernist had ever done. Among Catholics Sullivan was known as a "Unitarian," and among his Unitarian brothers he was known as a "Catholic," But Sullivan's Unitarian religion was very different from traditional Unitarian postures. Catholic elements transformed the conventional liberal stance. He did not believe in the current worship of modern science. He believed that there was a most disillusioning collapse of moral standards. And he cautioned against the growing dominance of secular subjects in Unitarian pulpits. In other areas of theology, he still believed in the historicity of the resurrection. He argued that creeds could make no claims to universality, but the message of Christ could. It was a message of beauty, but it was also a message of the cross.

When he became the pastor of All Souls, Sullivan insisted that the liberal church needed a greater development of personal spirituality. He felt that God was the only subject for preaching. He insisted on the primacy of Christ as a means to a true understanding of Deity. The new breed of Unitarians often admitted that they believed in God, but when pressed they were apt to be found to believe that "Man is God." Sullivan called this an insane perversion of the liberal position.

William Sullivan was often as critical of his own church as his former one. John Clarence Petrie, who also made the pilgrimage from Catholicism to Unitarianism, met Dr. Sullivan when as a Catholic he met him at meetings at the Layman's League at All Souls Church. Petrie wrote of him shortly after Sullivan's death:

> *Dr. Sullivan's discontent with things as he saw them in our liberal churches is in no wise to be interpreted as any desire on his part to leave our fellowship or look with envy elsewhere. Cheap as he felt we had become at times, it was nothing as compared with the slavery of mind he saw in orthodox churches. . . . Sullivan was a splendid example of Augustine's truth that man cannot be satisfied with anything here below because nothing here below is big enough to fill the heart of man, which is destined for Infinity.(38)*

Sullivan's Christology

Towards the end of his life he began to speak in prophetic accents. He had attempted to find a balance between the optimism and belief in progress characteristic of early-twentieth-century America and the older ideas of moral responsibility. In place of a balance many times he believed that he had produced a paradox. He believed on one hand that man could eventually triumph over materialism and skepticism. He foresaw some kind of salvation within history, a salvation that would be universal and collective.

Sullivan's Christology was also an attempt to blend traditional and modern, Catholic and liberal. It tended to oscillate between mysticism and moralism, naturalism and supernaturalism. Trinity Godheads he could not understand, but he respected those who held these beliefs, so long as they were not hypocritical. He did not believe, like Dr. Albert Schweitzer, that the historical Jesus could not be known. He did not believe that Christ is the Redeemer taught by Protestant and Catholic theology, but he believed that the Christ involved the temporal in the eternal, without compromising the eternal by the temporal. Just as certainly as prophets are sent to earth to speak of immortal issues, so Jesus of Nazareth was sent to be the leader of mankind in the transfiguration of the world.

This then was the spiritual pilgrimage of this man who served All Souls as minister for six years, a pilgrimage almost certainly unique in the annals of American religion.

His literary contributions also were outstanding. We have already mentioned several of his books; *Letters to His Holiness Pope Pius X, The Priest,* his novel, *From the Gospel to the Creeds,* and *Readings for Meditation.* Published posthumously was a semi-autobiography called *Under Orders,* later republished by the Beacon Press.

An Appreciation

Dr. Sullivan was one of the most eloquent men ever yet to occupy a Unitarian pulpit in the United States. Samuel A. Eliot said of him; "The old found him tender and full of courtesy, the young were sure of his understanding sympathy, and yielded him a pure devotion,"(39) Charles H. Strong said of him; "His peril lay in the danger that he might have foundered and never reached shore. But, after a period of bewilderment and dismay, he had found what he sought."(40) Dr. Minot Simons, his successor, said of him; "Coming from a church of absolute spiritual authority, he gloried in the truth which had made him free.(41)

The tablet dedicated to Dr. Sullivan on the north wall of the present church sanctuary, reads in part; "He forsook the shelter of authority in the perilous search for truth."

Dr. William Sullivan was stricken with a fatal bout of pneumonia while on vacation in Maine in the fall of 1935. His passing was mourned by many in many churches. Dr. Ratte says of him:

Though Sullivan prospered as a man, in marriage, in financial security, in personal recognition, in a limited range of literary

activity, he remained dissatisfied theologically with all church-
es. As a seminarian and as a young priest, he had showed
some insight into the contradictions of Roman Catholicism in a
democratic and pluralistic setting, and he had also responded,
though with little originality, to the European discovery of the
vast distance between Catholicism and the secular epoch. As a
mature minister and preacher, he reacted strongly against the
extensions of the political and scientific directions with which
Modernism had hoped to reconcile the traditional Church, Pa-
triotism, militant theism, and an ultimately dulling rhetorical
enthusiasm.(42)

I have often wondered as I have looked at that tablet so many
times if Dr. Sullivan had lived in our times with the rapid shifting of ideas within the Roman Catholic Church, would we ever
have had the gift of his sweet spirit and dynamic convictions
within the Unitarian ranks? He kept an emotional loyalty to the
religion in which he had been bred, and he brought to his new
faith of Unitarianism a conviction that few of us can equal or
express so eloquently.

When the tablet to William Laurence Sullivan was unveiled
on March 26, 1939. Dr. Minot Simons, then the minister of All
Souls, said of him:

He brought to us a spirit a flame with the divine fire of truth. Dr.
Sullivan was made of martyr stuff. He had a divine consecration
which in former ages led to crucifixion, to the stake, to pains and
sufferings unspeakable, and to joys ineffable. Even in this age he
had to face and to endure in the process of his conversion, inner
struggles and sadnesses and outer opposition and ostracism. An
extraordinary tribute, however, came from a group of his former
Catholic students. They agreed that Dr. Sullivan, more than any
other living man, incarnated for them the spirit of Christ. With a
price, he achieved his freedom.(43)

Minot Osgood Simons. Sixth Minister of All Souls (1923-1941)

CHAPTER 4

A Builder Arrives:

The Ministry of Minot Osgood Simons (1923-1941)

Life is an incarnation of mystery because in and through it are the manifestations of infinities. The more we discover the more we are made to realize that there is yet more to know, infinitely more. . . Our comprehension is along finite lines. What we have to do is to take an attitude so positive and so high-minded that we shall be true to our own highest ideals and thus, in spite of the mystery, achieve the best results in life.(1)

Minot Simons

The church had proceeded almost immediately to seek to find a successor for Dr. Sullivan. But they had no success in attaining unanimity in their choice.

Various Candidates Considered

As early as the end of January 1922, the trustees had decided to ask Rev. Abbot Peterson of Brookline, Massachusetts, to preach as a candidate at one of the Sunday morning services in February. Also two trustees were appointed to go to St. Paul, Minnesota, to hear the Rev. Frederick May Eliot. The name of Dr. William H. Faunce, the president of Brown University, was also suggested as a candidate.

Certainly the church was aiming high in their list of possible successors. One of the problems of being very specific about this period of the calling of a new minister is that there are no minutes extant for this period as there are no minutes until the annual meeting, early in 1923. The minutes of the meeting on February

10 suggest that Rudolph Kissel, the president of the board, was confined to his home by illness. But it must be presumed that the board would have met in spite of a lack of minutes.

What transpired about the candidacy of Abbot Peterson is not known, as we do not have the Sunday calendars until1923. It was stated later that both president Faunce of Brown University, and another candidate, Professor Theodore Soares of the University of Chicago, were not interested because "they could not give up their professorships with the respect of pensions, to preach in a church."(2) Nor was Reverend Frederick May Eliot interested in being considered as a candidate for the New York church since he was very happy in St. Paul.

This was the state of affairs when Dr. Sullivan introduced his bombshell proposal that there be a Board of Preachers. But this idea was not acceptable. One thing that the church did not consider, and evidently Dr. Sullivan failed to appreciate also, was the fact that men trained for the ministry in those days had an idea that preaching was a very important part of their profession, and the idea of being an "executive secretary" to a church would not appeal to top notch ministers in the denomination. Perhaps these rather prominent preachers and teachers were not enamored of the idea of the Board of Preachers as a plan for their future.

In any case after Dr. Samuel A. Eliot's visit, and when the options were again presented, the congregation was moved to take some action. Dr. Eliot had even told the meeting that the Unitarian Association would not object if a minister was called from another denomination, a startling suggestion for a denominational official. The congregation then put an end to the options by voting to empower the trustees to get down to business, to locate a suitable Unitarian candidate, and to report back to the congregation when they had found such a candidate.

The new board of trustees had Lawrence Billings as president and Lawrance I. Neale, a prominent layman in the congregation, was elected vice president. Charles P. Blaney was made treasurer although at first he refused the position. The board was divided on many issues. The contested positions of the officers on the board of trustees showed that there was dissension in the church. But perhaps the presence of the first two women trustees helped with the feeling of unity. Miss Schuyler attended every meeting until her death, and Mrs. McGinley was present most of the time.

Settling on Simons

The first indication that Dr. Minot Simons was under consideration came at a meeting which was held on March 13. Lawrance Neale reported that Mr. Billings had talked with Dr. Samuel A. Eliot about the possibility of securing the services of Dr. Minot Simons who was serving on the staff of the Unitarian Association. Mr. Neale was appointed to interview Dr. Simons, and to offer him a salary of $8,000. But Mr. Neale did not get a favorable response from Dr. Simons. He was working for the nationwide denomination in his position as head of the Department of Church Extension, which he conceived to be a very important task. Still Dr. Simons did promise Mr. Neale to give careful consideration until he was to preach again at All Souls on Sunday, March 25.

After this preaching engagement, Mr. Neale again had conversations with Dr. Simons, and he finally consented to come to All Souls if the congregation should extend a call. The salary was to be $9,000 per year, a secretary for the office was to be employed, and a parish assistant was to be considered. There was general rejoicing within the Society. Mr. Billings, the retiring president of the board of trustees, promised a gift of $6,137.32, which was the amount of the deficit the previous year. The board was appreciative, and Mr. Neale was elected as president.

The special meeting of the congregation took place on April 16, 1923, and there was the anticipated concurrence of the congregation in the selection of Dr. Simons. He was to begin his duties in September. At the same time the congregation indicated that they would employ a secretary, that a parish worker was desperately needed, and that a new site ought to be found to relocate the church. The congregation was not alone in feeling that they had made the right choice. Dr. Sullivan wrote; "the church will have a zealous and able minister in Dr. Simons. It is an excellent choice. I do not know where you could have made a better one. My best wish is for his success and the church's progress with him."(3) Dr. Francis Greenwood Peabody, the old friend of the church, wrote; "I have for more than a year regarded Minot Simons as the best possible choice for your beloved church."(4)

Dr. Samuel A. Eliot, commended "my dear colleague 'Simons' to the church. He has just the gifts of mind and heart that you need. You have made the best choice possible, and we all anticipate the renewed vitality of All Souls and the steady increase of the church in stability and members under Simon's inspiring leadership."(5)

The installation of Minot Simons as the sixth minister of All Souls Church took place on Sunday evening, November 4, 1923. The installation committee had George F. Baker as honorary chair man, and Laurance I. Neale as chairman. There is a long list of guests of honor, including most of the Unitarian ministers in the New York City area.

Walter Reid Hunt, Field Secretary of the American Unitarian Association, gave the invocation. Dr. John Howland Lathrop of the Brooklyn Church read the scripture lesson and gave the installation prayer. Laurance I. Neale led the congregation in the service of installation. The address for the evening was given by Edwin Francis Gay, formerly the dean of the Graduate School of Business Administration at Harvard, formerly a member of the War Trade Board, and now President of the New York Evening Post. Dr. Gay was a most distinguished Unitarian layman, and the father of Edward R. Gay, who was active in the church in my time. William Laurence Sullivan gave the charge to the minister and the people. Dr. Samuel A. Eliot gave a second address, and Dr. Simons, pronounced the benediction. It was the beginning of a significant ministry and a period of great progress for All Souls Church.

The Sixth Minister

Dr. Minot Osgood Simons came from a New England back ground. As far back as 1635, the records show that one of his ancestors, William Simons, ran the ferry, and performed public functions in the town of Ipswich, Massachusetts. Minot Osgood Simons was born in Manchester, New Hampshire, on September 24, 1868, the son of Langdon Simons and Sarah Frances Fifield. Osgood was a family name, and Minot Simons continued to use it until he was nearly fifty years of age, abandoning it then for convenience in writing. He was an only child, and when he was sixteen years of age his father, who was a jeweler, died. He lived thereafter at the home of his paternal grandfather. He attended Manchester High School and spent a year at Phillips Exeter Academy, and entered Harvard College in the fall of 1887. He was a diligent student, but also found time to play on the baseball team. He was popular with his classmates and graduated in the class of 1891.

He continued his education at the Harvard Divinity School, finishing his work three years later in 1894. On December 18, 1894, in Boston, he married Helen Louise Savage, daughter of Dr. Minot J. Savage. Not only was his wife the daughter of a famous Unitarian minister, but her brother was Reverend Dr. Maxwell Savage, my predecessor in the Second Parish in the Town of Worcester, Massachusetts. They had one son, Langdon Savage Simons.

Minot Simons began his ministry in the old First Parish Church of Billerica, Massachusetts, in January, 1895. H remained in this small and typical New England parish for five years. He was then called to the Cleveland, Ohio, church where he served for 19 years. In Cleveland he was literally all things to all people. He relocated the old church and lcd the congregation in building a new edifice in what was then a fine residential section of Cleveland. H was concerned with and active in almost every good cause in the community.

In 1919, he responded to a call from Dr. Samuel A. Eliot to

come to Boston to be on the headquarters staff of the American Association to be in charge of the Department of Church Extension. He had been in this position only four years when he accepted the call to come to All Souls. In 1921, Meadville Theological School had conferred on him the degree of Doctor of Divinity (D.D.).

Thus, Dr. Simons began his work at All Souls not as an inexperienced young man as great many of his predecessors had been, but as a man fully qualified to lead the church into a new era. He had been chosen by Dr. Eliot to be the Director of the Department of Extension because he had some very fine qualifications and it was these qualities in Dr. Simons that were to enable him to lead All Souls into a new era of expansion. For this purpose, he needed some full-time assistance by adding to the church staff.

Starting In

In line with the agreement which the congregation had made with Dr. Simons, the trustees now proceeded to set up an office with a full time secretary. On October 7, Mrs. Harold Sichel's name appears as church secretary, and by the first of October the position of parish assistant was filled with the arrival of Miss Louise D. Henderson. Her work was to be primarily with the Sunday School and the organizations. In January, 1925, Mrs. Sichel was replaced by Dorothy Osborn who served in this capacity for some years. In the fall of 1935, Miss Elizabeth L. Reed be came the "Supervisor of Religious Education," a new title designed to replace that of parish assistant. She served in this capacity until 1944.

All Souls had a distinguished preacher on May 24, 1924. when Dr. L. P. Jacks, the head of Manchester College, Oxford, and the editor of *The Hibbert Journal,* occupied the pulpit. On May 11, Dr. Arthur Cushman McGiffert, the President of Union Theological Seminary, was the preacher of the day.

The year 1924 was also an eventful one because George F. Baker, an All Souls trustee, gave 5 million dollars to the Harvard Business School to build the original campus across the Charles River from Harvard College. The story, which may be apocryphal, was told that at first he refused to give a million dollars, and the Harvard agent who had approached him did not under stand that he wanted to give the entire sum needed. On June 24, 1926, Harvard University conferred the honorary degree of Doctor of Laws (LL.D) on him. He had not only a distinguished banking career, but he had been most generous to many institutions of higher learning in addition to Harvard.

All Souls Church lost two distinguished women, the Schuyler sisters, early in Dr. Simons' ministry. Georgina and Louisa Lee Schuyler were the granddaughters of George Lee Schuyler and Eliza Hamilton Schuyler, and the great-granddaughters of Alexander Hamilton and Major General Philip Schuyler. Schuyler had served in the French and Indian War from 1755 until 1760, and then had been a Major General in the Continental Army and had organized the attack on Canada, although he did not lead it. He was a member of the Continental Congress, one of the first two senators from New York State (1789-1791, 1797-1798), and supported aggressively the programs of his son-in-law, Alexander Hamilton.

Georgina Schuyler died on Christmas morning, 1923, in her eighty-third year. She was one of the first two women elected to the board of trustees in 1923. She had attended Christmas services only two days before her death.

Louisa Lee Schuyler was the more famous of the two sisters. She outlived her sister a few years, but she had poor health for a long time. She passed away at the home of J. P. Morgan in Highland Falls, New York, on October 10, 1926. Her name appears in the Sunday School records as early as 1845. As a young woman she had organized the New York Division of the United States Sanitary Commission, "The Women's Central," as it was called. She was the founder of the State Charities Aid Association of New York, and she was a leader in the movement that led to the removal of the insane from county poorhouses to state hospitals. She organized the first training school for nurses in the United States at Bellevue Hospital in New York City, and organized a committee of physicians and laymen to establish the organization for the blind which is now known as "The Lighthouse."

Both of these distinguished ladies were buried with services from All Souls. Both of their services were conducted jointly by Dr. Simons and Dr. Francis Greenwood Peabody, and both were buried in the family plot at Sleepy Hollow Cemetery in Tarrytown, New York.

Celebrations and Innovations

During the Lenten Season in 1925, thirty-three Lenten services were held during lunch hour in the hope of attracting people who worked in the vicinity of the church.

On October 11, 1925, the final meeting of the National Conference of Unitarian Churches was held in Cleveland, Ohio. This event was noted in the church calendar because Dr. Henry Bellows had been instrumental in organizing the National Conference in 1865 just as the Civil War was ending. The church calendar for that week stated: "His experience with the Sanitary Commission had created a strong faith within him that liberal religion could do much more effective work if it were better organized, and the leadership which he himself had displayed during the war led the Unitarians to accept his leadership along the lines which he had suggested." A note was appended to the notice in the calendar; "It is hoped that All Souls will be represented at this last meeting of the conference." The National Conference was merged with the American Unitarian Association, and the A.U.A thus became for the first time an organization of churches rather than just an organization of individuals.

On December 20, 1925, the 70th anniversary of the dedication of the Twentieth Street Church was celebrated. The church, better known as "The Church of the Holy Zebra," because of its

The brownstone building at the future site of All Souls Church at Eightieth and Lexington Avenue.

horizontal stripes of red brick and limestone, had been dedicated on Christmas Day, 1855, by Dr. Bellows.

Relocating

The most important concern for the church was that the church building needed to be relocated. Serious discussion of this matter had been considered on April 9, 1926, at a special meeting of the congregation. When the church building was erected in 1855, the area around Gramercy Park was a growing residential one. But the migration of the population northward on Manhattan Island had been rapid, and many of the parishioners now had to travel a great distance to the services. It was obvious to almost all of the parishioners that the church ought to move further uptown.

Dr. Simons had relocated the Cleveland church, and had helped to supervise the construction of the new building before he went to Boston to work in church extension for the denomination. Dr. Simons realized, as did most of the parishioners, that the site at 20th Street was totally unsatisfactory. The move must be above Sixtieth Street and probably as far north as Eightieth Street. The congregation continued through the nineteen-twenties to grapple with this problem at every opportunity.

It is sometimes difficult to understand the extent of the problem of land values that were involved. The value of the Twentieth Street property had declined over the years, and land as far north as Eightieth Street was very expensive. If the old church could be sold for enough to buy the new land, and only the land, the church would be fortunate indeed. In addition, there would be the expense of erecting the new edifice.

In March of 1926, the trustees discussed the advisability of purchasing the Park Avenue Baptist Church on Park Avenue and Sixty-Fourth Streets which was now on the market. The church had been completed only a few years previously for Dr. Harry Emerson Fosdick, largely through the generosity of John D. Rockefeller, a member of the church. Now this congregation was moving north to

Riverside Drive to build a larger church, actually a great cathedral, to accommodate the crowds that Dr. Fosdick was drawing. There was the possibility of buying this beautiful Park Avenue edifice, but the building could not be occupied until 1928, and the price was high. But it was an attractive new building, and if the trustees knew then what they were later to learn, they would have been well advised to buy this church as a bargain. The congregation met and discussed the matter. George R. Bishop, the unofficial historian of the church, was concerned that there would not be a place for the St. Gaudens bas-relief sculpture of Henry Bellows, and that the pews would be uncomfortable. Dr. Simons assured him that there would be a place for "Dear Bellows."

Later when the board met they decided to let the Baptists know that they were vitally interested, but not to make an offer at that time. What happened in regard to the purchase of the property is not clear, except that the Presbyterians bought the church and All Souls did not. The price of one and a quarter million dollars seemed to be excessive in the minds of the All Souls trustees, and yet that was almost exactly what the new church which was soon to be built was to cost.

A special meeting of the congregation was called for November 7, 1928. Rudolph Neuendorffer, as chairman of the policy committee, gave a report on the status of relocating the church. The final decision on the area of relocation, he said, had been between 59th and 86th Streets, and between Lexington Avenue and the East River. Both Park and Fifth Avenues had been eliminated because of the cost. A satisfactory plot had been located on the southeast corner of Lexington Avenue and 80th Street. An option to the property had been secured. The price of the property was $625,000, with a cash payment of $231,000, and a long-term mortgage for the balance. Mr. Neuendorffer stated that the committee had promises of two $100,000 gifts, and $300,000 had been promised for the "Removal Fund." The present church property, he believed, would realize $100,000 to $150,000 in cash, and a mortgage of about $400,000. Thus it was felt that the society had in hand about a million dollars with which to make their plans. He recommended that favorable action be taken.

Seven men and two women then spoke favorably upon the subject. Even George Bishop, who could now forsee ample space for his cherished St. Gaudens bas-relief and more comfortable pews, spoke in favor of the move. A written ballot was taken, showing 82 votes for and none against the move. Thus the society embarked upon its new venture unanimously, a courageous thing for eighty-two people to do. So the lot was purchased and the planning went ahead.

On December 17, 1928, at a meeting of the trustees, it was announced that Hobart Upjohn was recommended as the architect. Parker Morse Hopper, a member of the church and the editor of The Architectural Record, had made this recommendation. Mr. Upjohn accepted, was voted as architect, and Otto Langmann, a member of All Souls, was chosen as associate architect. There was some difficult in selling the 20th Street property, for it did not seem to be a desirable site once the property was put on the market. But it was sold to Henry A. Sherry, a real estate developer, for the sum of $475,000; $10,000 on signing the contract, $15,000 on May 2, 1929, $50,000 upon delivery of the deed, and a mortgage for $400,000. The society now decided to move to the MacDowell Club for Sunday services. The club was located at 166 East 73rd Street, and being in the vicinity of the new church area, was considered an appropriate site.

A farewell service was held in the "Church of the Holy Zebra" on June 9, 1929. It was a typical Sunday morning service such as had been conducted for the past seventy-five years in the same building. Dr. Simons spoke on "Retrospect." A group picture was taken on the steps outside the church after the service. Modern historians would be interested if a copy could be located. A copy of this photo was placed in the cornerstone of the new building. The order of service contained a brief history of the church, a brief history which was used again and again when special occasions were celebrated over the years. There was also a page and a half "Prospect ofn the New Church" which told the congregation about the new building:

The new church building will be a beautiful edifice. Colonial in design, with amble acommodations in the Paris House for the church activities including facilities for a modern school of religious education... The new church home will be comopleted by the addtion of a small chapel, one of the most useful and beautiful features of a city church.(6)

The Great Depression Intervenes

Meanwhile, the bubble of speculation that had been creating so much paper prosperity burst in one terrible day on Wall Street. October 24, 1929, is remembered as "Black Thursday," for on that day nearly everyone wanted to sell securities and no one wanted to buy them. Brokers wired their customers to ask for more money for margins. Many persons were completely wiped-out during the next week when demands were made for larger margins that investors could not raise. The "get-rich-quick" mania had afflicted almost everyone.

The only indication in the church minutes of what happened is that at meeting #6 of the trustees which unfortunately is not dated (one of the few minutes not dated) the president of the board authorized William B. Nichols, Lawrence I. Grinnell, and Wyman to form a committee to review the securities. Actually, it was it was not the church organization which suffered greatly from the steep decline in the market, for the church had a small investment portfolio. The problem was that the individuals within the church who had made pledges to move the church, had suffered. There was also concern about the property on 20th street which had been sold, and which soon had to be repossessed.

The buyer of this property had been wiped out by the crash othe market, and he could not fulfill his contracts with the church. Procedure to repossess was reluctantly voted on January 24, 1930, by the trustees. Otto Stansfield and Charles P. Blaney were empowered to foreclose. Then the trustees set about the almost impossible proposition of trying to sell the property again in the

the depths of what came to be known as "The Great Depression." Nevertheless, in spite of the bad economy, the Every Member Canvass for 1930 seemed to be within the possibility of realization with over $14,000 pledged. The board also voted that the 20th Street property should not be sold for less than $405,000.

In the early part of 1931, the depression was at its worst, nearly one in four men in New York City were out of work, and the city could scarcely collect its real estate taxes. This was not an auspicious time to erect a new church building. When the trustees met in February, 1931, Rudolph Neuendorffer presented a list of possibilities which the church could take now with regard to its properties, such as resale of the 80th Street property, building a basement with a temporary roof at 80th Street, and then building the church later, or even moving back to the 20th Street church.

The trustees rejected all of these propositions knowing that any of them would be a step backward for the re-location of the new church. It was now becoming apparent that the church would have to pay city real estate taxes on its old property which was now assessed for a value of $405,000, of which only $145,000 represented the value of the building. Then the trustees tried to borrow $300,000 at 5% interest from the American Unitarian Association, but this could not be arranged because the parent institution was also in financial trouble.

Going Ahead Anyway

Dr. Simons then announced a plan of underwriting that he had arranged with the George F. Baker estate. Mr. Baker had recently died in his 91st year, and his duties were now being renewed by his son, George F. Baker. (The Bakers never used the terms senior and junior.) The Baker Estate agreed to pay the interest for five years on such loans as the trustees must negotiate in order to complete the church building project. This amounted to a sum of approximately $20,000 a year. Dr. Simons announced this solid backing by the Bakers in the church calendar for May 31, telling the congregation that the Bakers' generous underwriting made it possible for the building at 80th Street to be commenced. During this year of 1931 not only Mr. Baker, who had been a trustee for fifty years, died, but also George R. Bishop, the unofficial historian, who had been a member of the board for almost forty years, also died. It was voted in July to abandon, for the present, consideration of the construction of the chapel and

The clay model of the proposed new church. Note the two build-ings in the foreground which were eliminated in the final plans because of cost.

parish house, and to move ahead with the construction of the church proper as soon as was possible.

Having abandoned the Twentieth Street Church in June, 1929, the congregation was meeting at the MacDowell Club on 73rd Street. The abandoned church, like most abandoned buildings, gradually became an eyesore to the community. Fortunately, the memorials so precious to Mr. Bishop had been removed and were in storage. Gradually the church became a place inhabited by the unemployed and those who were termed "Hoboes." It was decided to demolish the church in preparation for what the trustees hoped would be a parking lot, all attempts to sell it having proved fruitless. The contractors had started the not-so-easy process of demolition, some of the walls were three feet thick, when a fire broke out in the building about 11 A.M. on August 24, 1931.

The newspapers presumed the next day in lead articles that the fire had been started by a cigarette thrown by what one paper described as a "tramp," "unemployed man," and "two hoboes without homes." In the fierce blaze that ensued, the building was left only a ruined shell. It was difficult even for the roaring fire to reduce the three foot thick walls that architect Jacob Wrey Mould had constructed in his Romanesque basilica. It was one of the great fires of 1931, and unfortunately several firemen were injured by falling debris.

But the fire did prompt the church to appoint a building committee consisting of Wyman D. Herbert as chairman. The members appointed were: Elliott S. Benedict, Parker Morse Hopper (an architect), Mark W. Maclay, Laurance I. Neale, Dr. William B. Dunning, Rudolph Neuendorffer, and Dr. Simons, ex-officio.

Laying the Cornerstone

It was a deeply moving event and one of almost sheer faith which occurred on Sunday afternoon, February 7, 1932, when the congregation gathered at the site of the new church on Lexington Avenue at 80th Street for the laying of the cornerstone of the new building. There was an address by Minot Simons, and then the cornerstone was laid. Those who assisted were Mr. Herbert, chairman of the building committee, Mr. Neuendorffer, president of the board of trustees, and a representative of the contractors and builders, Cauldwell-Wingate Co. The contents of the cornerstone are listed in the church calendar for the following week, and they include sermons and other material, and the picture taken at the last

The new church building under construction.

The new building looking towards the pulpit.

The new building looking towards the rear organ gallery.

service of the entire congregation in front of the old church.

The bottom of the Depression was not yet in sight. It soon discovered that the taxes on the old church would amount to about $13,000 per year, largely on the value of the land rather than the destroyed building. The taxes were levied because a. church could not have an abatement on its property taxes on more than one piece of property. Dr. Simons, Miss Henderson, and Miss Osborn offered to take a salary cut because of the failure of the Every Member Canvass to meet its minimum goals, and cuts of 10% were authorized by the board as of July 1 for all employees.

There was an intense discussion about the locating of some of the memorials that had been put in storage after removal from the old church. The first decision about the Williams sculpture had been to locate it in the choir, but both Mrs. Williams and the sculptress objected to this as being too far from the congregation It was decided to locate it in its present spot on the north side near the front of the church under the window. The Austin Organ in the new church was the gift of Miss Louise E. von Bernuth in memory of her father and mother, Mr. and Mrs. Frederick A. von Bernuth, who had been members of the church for many years.

Work progressed nicely on the new building. There were no labor shortages in the bottom of the depression. The Dedication Service took place on Sunday evening, November 13, 1932. Those who gathered in the church that evening were thankful that in view of the economic situation there was a building to be dedicated at all, even though it lacked a parish house and the chapel for which the congregation had hoped. There was a distinguished committee for the dedication, and a distinguished list of the guests of honor, including most of the ministers of the area.

Dr. Frank Oliver Hall, the minister of the Church of the Divine Paternity (Fourth Universalist Church), New York, gave the invocation, led in the Lord's Prayer, and read the scripture lesson. Dr. Samuel Atkins Eliot, who by this time had moved from the presi dency of the American Unitarian Association to be the minister of the Arlington Street Church in Boston, gave

The Chancel of All Souls as it appeared for the first eight years. Dr. Simons and the Choir.

The Chancel as it appeared after the cross was erected in 1942.

the sermon. He spoke of the note of thanksgiving and rejoicing that was in all minds and hearts because of the completion of the house of worship. He reminisced about Dr. Henry Bellows, who was his uncle by marriage, and whom he had known as a boy. He reflected on the ministries of Theodore Williams, Thomas Slicer, and William Sullivan. He saluted the present leader, Dr. Simons, his former colleague. He recalled the memory of some of the trustees of the church whom he had known over the years. It was actually neither a great nor a profound sermon, but it contained the words of a loving friend of All Souls wishing them well in their new church home.(7)

Dr. Louis Craig Cornish, the successor to Dr. Eliot as the president of the American Unitarian Association, brought greetings. Then there were two addresses. Frederick Adrian Delano, formerly a member of the Federal Reserve Board whose family had long been connected with the church, gave one address; the second was given by the best known American preacher of the day, Dr. Harry Emerson Fosdick, minister of the Riverside Church in New York City. Many persons expressed surprise that the outstanding spokesman of a more orthodox denomination should have given this important address. The answer is quite simple; in 1932 Unitarians were more conservative than they are today, and Harry Emerson Fosdick well represented the "liberal" point of view in Protestantism to a great many of the American people. His choice was almost inevitable if there was not to be a Unitarian spokesman.

Dr. Simons called attention to the re-established memorials in the church. The delivery of the keys to the president of the board of trustees, Rudolph Neuendorffer, was made by Wyman Drummond Herbert, the chairman of the building committee, and then the congregation stood for an Act of Dedication. It was probably such a lengthy service by this time that the congregation was happy to rise. Dr. Simons gave a dedication prayer, and then a hymn composed by his father-in-law, Dr. Minot J. Savage, for the dedication of Dr. Simons former church in Cleveland, Ohio, was sung to conclude the service which ended with a benediction by Dr. Simons.

Description of the New Church

The edifice thus dedicated was designed by Hobart Upjohn, the architect, and Otto F. Langmann, the associate architect. Upjohn began his studies for the design of the new building with a picture of the site before the old brownstone apartments were razed. It was an unprepossessing site, but a good one, at the corner of Eightieth Street and Lexington Avenue. The lot was not large, scarcely over a hundred feet square. Then Mr. Upjohn studied some of the memorials which had to be accommodated in the new church.

There was a high pulpit at the rear of the chancel. There were problems in designing this because of the lack of depth in the lot. The small chapel that was specified was not built until 1953. Plans called for a chapel seating 75-100 (the present chapel seats 60). In the basement of the chapel there was to be a large vault with small compartments for the deposit of cinerary urns, or containers for human ashes. This plan had to be abandoned when it was discovered that there was a hard ledge of rock, and the blasting would be very expensive. The large room under the church was to seat 500 persons (It seats about 300). Plans called for a large sub-basement. But during early construction when the ledge of rock was discovered, the decision was made to heat the church with gas (then an expensive fuel, but requiring no storage tanks). In the light of the future economic developments, this turned out to be a matter of foresight.

There was also a description of the parish house, and plans were prepared for this addition which included an apartment for the sexton. It was a rather grandiose plan, and one wonders with the space available how all of this could have been accommodated, but the rock ledge, and the continuance of the depression put these ambitious plans on hold.

The architecture of the church building was discussed in an article in the January 1933 issue of *The Architectural Record,* with four pictures and a plan of the new church. Evidently many trial plans were made running from Italian Romanesque to variations of the Colonial style until the present plan was finally adopted. The tower, in order to meet New York City fire standards, had to be fireproof and made of stone. Many tons of Texas limestone were used to build a very high steeple which had the feeling of New England, and although taller buildings have recently been built within a block of the church, the tower still dominates the area as the architect had hoped that it would. The tower being made of steel, cement and stone is very heavy, and it was an architectural achievement to support this heavy tower. The interior of the church was treated with acoustical plaster, but the acoustics have always been a problem. It is difficult for the minister to be heard without a troubling echo. Today a second pulpit extending out into the body of the church has replaced the high pulpit as a place to preach sermons, and in many ways this has solved the long-standing acoustical problems.

The furniture of the church followed closely the precedents of colonial architecture with the pulpit placed in the center against the rear wall of the chancel. The pews were painted white with mahogany trim. The Austin Organ (replaced in 1989 with a new organ) was in the gallery at the rear of the church where a place was also provided for a large choir. The church seated 600 persons, which was the goal in the original planning of the building, and something far smaller than the approximately 1250 persons who could be seated in the 20th Street Church. The exterior of the church was built of common Hudson River brick. The entry hall of the vestibule was designed to imitate the "Federal Period" in American architecture.

All things considered the present church is a fine building and has stood the test of time admirably. This is the first of the four buildings that All Souls has built where the roof did not give trouble. It is of steel truss design so that there could be no rotting of timbers. With the later addition of two sections of the parish house in 1953 and 1961, it is an adequate church plant, and thus far no further additions are contemplated. The congregation to all intents and purposes made the decision in 1961 when the addition to Wiggin House was made, not to encroach on the beautiful Memorial Garden.

There is little prospect that moving any further north on the island of Manhattan would be of any advantage to the congregation's growh. The present church building is likely to serve all present needs, and future plans will more or less have to be tailored to the present plant. If the church at the moment has problems with the building they are the problems of the maintenance of any building. This is almost a new situation for the All Souls congregation whose other buildings have had many problems, most especially the 20th Street basilica.

The mood of the congregation in moving to the new location and their desire to appeal to those living in the East Side community is illustrated by a message of greeting which Dr. Simons wrote. This was printed as a message of welcome to visitors on a small brochure which also contained the architect's rendering of the new building. This message explained the philosophy of the Church of All Souls. It is interesting to read as it illustrates where the congregation was in its thinking at that point of time.

This church is dedicated to religion but not to a creed. Neither upon itself nor upon its members does it impose a test or doctrinal formula. Love to God and man and the perfecting of our spiritual nature it regards as the unchanging substance of religion and the essential gospel of Jesus. Consecrating itself to these principles, it aims at cultivating reverence for Truth, moral character and insight, helpfulness to humanity, and the spirit of communion with the Infinite. It welcomes to its worship and fellowship all who are in sympathy with a religion thus simple and thus free.

As a non-creedal church we hope to appeal to our new neighborhood as a Neighborhood Church. We hope to enlist the interest of all individuals and families who are not affiliated with some other church. We aspire to be a family

*church for parents who desire for themselves and for their
children the ministrations of a liberal religion.(8)*

Thus the church presented itself and its message to the East
Side community.

A "Free" Church

In the planning for the new church there had been a tacit
understanding that the church was gradually moving toward the
policy of a "free church," that is, the pews would not be rented
as in past buildings, but they would be open to everyone at every
service. There were many members of the congregation who still
felt that it would be an advantage and convenience to have their
own reserved family pew for services. Recognizing that this feeling still existed, a committee which reported in December 1932
summarized the future policy of the church. Persons who rented
pews in the old church were to be accorded that privilege in the
new church. But such pews were not to be held after the service
had been in progress for ten minutes.(9)

This policy led gradually to the point when there were no pews
reserved. This was the end of a practice which had existed since
the congregation occupied its first building in 1821. The Every
Member Canvass replaced pew rentals as a way of raising annual
budgets. In some churches there was a deeding of the pews to a
group of trustees. But at All Souls the change was made gradually
and by an evolutionary process until today it is a "free church" in
this sense of the term.

A rather unique service took place on Sunday morning March
26, 1933. Minot Simons spoke at the morning service on the life of
Joseph Priestley on the occasion of the two hundredth anniversary
of his birth in 1733. Priestley was an ardent British Unitarian minister as well as one of the great scientists of the eighteenth century.
Simons spoke of Priestley not only as the discoverer of oxygen,
but also as the discoverer of soda water, nitric acid, nitrous oxide,

hydrogen chloride, ammonia, and sulphur dioxide. After the service the congregation was invited to assemble in Fellowship Hall where Wyman D. Herbert, lately chairman of the building committee, repeated Priestley's experiment in creating oxygen and explained its significance. As we have seen in Volume I of the All Souls history, when Joseph Priestley first came to New York City in 1794 fleeing religious persecution in England, he was welcomed by the populace and the heads of government. But he was never invited to preach in any church in New York City for his religious ideas were considered to be too radical.(10)

Financial Problems

By the beginning of 1934 as the depression deepened, the church's finances also were in deep trouble. The church budget for the year was $65,000 of which two-thirds or $40,000 was for taxes and mortgage interest. This meant that there was very little money to keep the church running. This compared, for example, in the 150th year of the church in 1969 when the budget was $219,000, of which no money whatsoever went for taxes and mortgage payments. This bad situation was alleviated some what when George F. Baker took over the interest payments on the 20th Street property.

The church had a debt to the First National Bank in the amount of $184,000, which had been loaned by the bank on a mortgage on the 20th Street property, and guaranteed by Mr. Baker. But taxes had been allowed to accumulate. Mr. Baker died in 1937, and by this time the amount of money owed on the note with interest and taxes amounted to almost $223,000. The Baker Estate Trustees were most generous when they agreed to take over the property (which would probably not sell for more than $150,000) in return for a cancellation of the mortgage. Thus ended a serious problem in that the church owned two churches, both highly mortgaged, and the 20th Street property seemed to be unsaleable. This bad situation was made palatable only because of the generosity of the two George F. Bakers and the trustees of the estate.

During this period it also became apparent that the church could not make the payments of interest to the Franklin Savings Bank which held the mortgage on the new church. In recognition of this fact, the bank reduced the mortgage interest to a rate of 2 3/4% per annum. This situation deteriorated until the "Burn the Mortgage Campaign" in 1944-1945 when the church finally paid off its burdensome debt.

Fortunately the church had in its leadership at this time two men who understood these business problems. Dr. Simons was a builder of churches, and Laurance I. Neale was a business-man who was gradually spending more and more time on church business. However, Dr. Simons was often weak and confined to his home because of illness. Mr. Neale was always at his side, having finally given up his business connections, and thus was able to devote more time to the church affairs. In addition, the church had the help of able laymen on its board of trustees; such men as Mark Maclay, Rudolph Neuendorffer, and Elliott Bene-dict, who knew business methods, and of course, the angels, the two George F. Bakers.

Symbolism Debated

Eight years after the church was dedicated it seemed to Dr. Si-mons that the large white panel of the sounding board behind the pulpit needed some sort of symbolism. The early pictures taken after the dedication show that this panel at first was simply a white wall the same color as the rest of the woodwork. Then a dark ma-roon cloth was hung in this space. Dr. Simons wrote in the calen-dar for Easter Sunday of 1940; "It is an interesting coincidence that the Cross which was in the old church is being restored in our new Church during the week before the Good Friday service, when we commemorate the supreme example before all the world of the sacrificial life."(11)

Actually, it was not really a coincidence at all, for Dr. Simons explained that following his recommendation a unanimous motion of the standing committee voted to install the Cross. It is an interesting fact in the history of the church that such an important decision about religious symbolism should be made by the standing committee in which the board of trustees concurred, rather than by the congregation itself. If there had been any great objection, which evidently there was not, there would have been repercussions at the next meeting of the society. There were none. We shall see that during the later years of my tenure and the early years of Forrester Church's tenure, this matter took six or seven years of discussion by the congregation to reach the present solution on symbolism.

Dr. Simons had a simple meaning for the symbolism of the cross, but it was not necessarily the interpretation that would be read into the symbol by other persons. He wrote:

As a liberal Christian church, we reinterpret the meaning of the Cross by regarding it as a symbol of the sacrificial character of all human lives sooner or later. All of us are called upon for sacrificial living and perhaps dying, as the years go by, and thus from the liberal point of view, the Cross has the inspiration of a universal instead of an individual meaning. As the Cross is the symbol of universal Christianity, it becomes a comfort and a spiritual stimulation to those who are endeavoring to live life triumphantly through sacrifice.

Dr. Simons continued his explanation:

All religious symbols appeal through sight to insight concerning needs which cannot wholly be put into words. They become outward and visible signs of inward and unutterable feelings, and so the Cross is restored to the Church for its ministration to those who feel encouraged, guided, and inspired by it."(12)

If any further explanation is needed after these words it

must be remembered that Europe was plunged into war at this time, Great Britain was threatened by a Nazi invasion, and America itself was not too far away from entering the war where sacrifice would be the order of the day. In addition, Dr. Simons himself, suffering from an incurable cancer, must have felt inwardly the need to sacrifice his own strength for the welfare of his beloved church.

Last Months

At the beginning of the fall season in 1940, Dr. Simons preached on November 24, but he was absent from the pulpit all of the month of December. The board granted him a leave of absence for the month of December because he was so seriously ill. Guest preachers filled the pulpit, and a notice in the calendar stated that "Mr. Laurance I. Neale will be at the Church Office every day, where he may be consulted about any matter."(13)

Mr. Neale himself delivered the Christmas sermon on December 22. But January did not see the return of the beloved Dr. Simons to the pulpit, and Mr. Neale preached again that month as did Mark Maclay, the president of the board of trustees. Guest preachers continued throughout February. The church calendar for February 23 contained the announcement that Dr. Simons had undergone an operation at New York Hospital on Monday, February 10. His progress was announced as "satisfactory," and it was stated that he would leave the hospital in a few weeks. But the seriousness of his condition was indicated in that persons were asked not to visit him. Visitors continued in the pulpit, and Laurance I. Neale preached again on Easter Sunday on April 11. He preached again on May 11.

The condition of Dr. Minot Simons was now so serious that a notice went out for a congregational meeting on May 19 for the purpose of calling an associate minister. At this meeting, as was expected, Laurance I. Neale was elected to be the associate minister. Mr. Neale was a businessman until the depression blotted out his position, and he had had no training for the ministry except as he had seen what happened first hand as the president of the board of trustees. On May 25, a prominent member of the church, Vilhajalmur Stefansson, the famous arctic explorer, preached the sermon.

Early on that Sunday morning while Mr. Steffansson was preaching in his pulpit, Dr. Minot Simons died at his home. Funeral services were held in the church on Tuesday, May 27, conducted by the Rev. Frederick May Eliot, the man who would not consider a call to All Souls nineteen years previously. Dr. Eliot was now the president of the American Unitarian Association. Mr. Neale assisted with the service. It was announced that the regular morning service in memory of Dr. Simons. Mr. Neale preached a sermon titled simply "Minot Simons." It was largely a biographical memoir which was used later in the biography of Minot Simons in Volume 4 of Heralds of a Liberal Faith, edited by Samuel A. Eliot.

Mr. Neale wrote:

He was a builder. He built this beautiful Church in which we are now assembled; he built the lovely house of worship in Cleveland, where he was minister for nineteen years; and scattered all over the country are churches started by his initiative and made strong by his energy.(14)

But in addition to being a builder he had occupied many positions of duty and honor. Dr. Simons had been a member of the board of preachers of Harvard University and a trustee of the Meadville Theological School, Phillips Exeter Academy and Hackley School. He was the permanent treasurer of his college class, twice a member of the board of managers of the Harvard Club of New York, a member of the board of overseers of Harvard University, the only minister ever to be elected president of the Associated Harvard Clubs. He had served his university and his denomination well.

Laurance Irving Neale. Seventh Minister of All Souls (1942-1955)

CHAPTER 5

A Preacher From The Pews:

*The Ministry of Laurance Irving Neale
(1942-1955)*

> *The church is not a useless institution, and it must not be
> al lowed ever to become such. It is the best instrument we
> have, or probably shall have. . . to give men a sense of
> harmony with the Eternal Spirit and with their fellow men,
> for which they long, and hence bring to them peace which
> is beyond understanding. It is also the best means that we
> know to create the vision of a better world.(1)*
>
> Laurance Irving Neale

By March of 1941 it was evident to almost everyone that Dr.
Simons was too ill to ever return to his duties as minister of the
church. In the meantime Mr. Neale had been filling in almost full
time for his beloved minister in every way that he could. Since he
was not an ordained minister he could not perform weddings, so
he would make all of the arrangements and then bring in one of the
neighboring ministers to perform the ceremony. He assisted in the
morning worship services on Sundays, preaching occasionally. He
made some parish calls, held office consultations, and arranged
for visiting ministers to occupy the pulpit. The attendance averaged 121 persons during January.

Acting Minister

Mr. Neale was able to conduct funeral services even though he was not ordained, and reported he had four funerals in February. The trustees extended Dr. Simons leave of absence, and then they considered the status of Mr. Neale and his compensation. Laurance Neale was very insistent that his services for December, January, and February be a gift to the church. But the trustees decided that he should have the status of acting minister which would be retroactive to December 1, 1940, and that his compensation would be fixed at $200 per month. By March of 1941, the board was so pleased with Mr. Neale's Easter sermon that they appropriated $35 to have it printed.

The new acting minister, Laurance Irving Neale, was the son of George F. Neale who came to America from England. An expert in glass-making, he was the first person to make plate glass in the United States. His mother's family had been Unitarians for generations. Originally they had been residents of Scituate, Massachusetts. Laurance was the fifth child born to George and Mary Adelaide Stetson Neale on July 20, 1885 in Boston, Massachusetts. Of these five children, only Laurance, Mary, and Alice lived to adulthood. Alice, his sister was active for many years at All Souls, passing away in 1956, the same year as her brother Laurance.

When Laurance was six months old the family moved to Saint Louis, Missouri, and after another dozen years the family moved to Allegheny, outside of Pittsburgh, where Laurance attended Shady Side Academy. In September of 1902 he entered Harvard College. He spent four happy years there, and was active in the Mandolin Club, the Hasty Pudding Club, and the student news paper, *The Harvard Crimson.*

It was upon his graduation from Harvard that Laurance Neale first came to New York City, which was to be his home for the remainder of his life. His first position was with the George F. Fuller Construction Company. After two years there he moved to J. B. King and Company, manufacturers of gypsum products.

While working at this company he attended law school at night. Although he never took the bar examination, he was helped in later years by this study of the law.

The First World War found Laurance Neale in service with the 15th Company, Plattsburg Training Regiment. He served in the168th Infantry from 1917 until 1919, and saw much action with troops of the Iowa National Guard, a part of the famous Rainbow Division. His friends said that Laurance went away to war as a rather happy-go-lucky fellow, but that he returned in a very serious mood, and that he never cared to discuss his war experiences.

Neale returned to work with J. B. King and Company, and he entered the sales field. In 1924 this firm was absorbed by the United States Gypsum Company, and Mr. Neale was transferred to Chicago where he organized and managed two new departments. In 1927 he resigned from the U.S. Gypsum Co. to become New York division sales manager of the Atlantic Gypsum Products Co. In 1930 he became vice president of the company. In 1930 he also married Loretta Adamson of New York City. His friends had joked with him about being a perennial bachelor. But in "Lolly," as Loretta Adamson was fondly called, he found a companion who stood by his side through much happiness and many difficult times. I was told that Mrs. Neale was called "Lolly" because she always had a lollypop in her pocketbook for any child who came along. I cannot vouch for the truth of this story. In 1936 in the middle of the great depression, the Atlantic Gypsum Co. was absorbed by the National Gypsum Co. None of the officers of Mr. Neale's firm continued as officers under the new arrangements. There simply was not enough construction taking place during the depression to keep all of the people in this particular industry employed, and Mr. Neale joined the ranks of the unemployed.

Since coming to New York City, Laurance Neale had been active in the affairs of All Souls Church. He served on the board of trustees three times. In 1937 he was elected a trustee for the fourth time, and successively was vice president, and then president of the board. As Dr. Simons health deteriorated, Mr. Neale having the time, became more and more involved in the running of the church. After his company was absorbed and he was without a job, he spent a year at Union Theological Seminary in New York City, partly to fill in the time, and partly because he had always had such a keen interest in the intellectual side of religion. With the increasing seriousness of Dr. Simon's illness he was appointed the acting minister from the fall of 1940 until he was appointed associate minister in 1941.

On April 29, 1941, Mark Maclay reported to the trustees tha-the had visited Dr. Simons who had suggested that Mr. Neale be given the title of assistant minister, that approval of his ordination should be obtained from the American Unitarian Association, and that an ordination and installation service should be held soon. Mr. Maclay received the unanimous endorsement of the standing committee for this process, and he discussed it with Mr. Neale: with the express understanding that, irrespective of what precise title might be conferred upon him, there should not be any obligation or expectation involved on the part of Mr. Neale, the board, or the Society, that by reason of such title or such call and ordination, Mr. Neale be considered Dr. Simons' successor.

The board then approved this matter in principle and set a meeting of the congregation for May 19.

Moving Up to Associate

Between the time that the board met and made this decision and the time that they met again on May 8, the matter had expanded so that Laurance Neale was to be called associate minister. In the light of the later confusion and controversy about this matter it is well to see that this change from assistant to associate minister was a logical change. In normal practice the board of trustees itself had the power to appoint an assistant minister. But if the congregation was to act upon the matter, and particularly if they were to ordain Mr. Neale to be a minister, there would have to be the consent of the congregation. An associate minister could be called only by the congregation, and since the congregation had to do the ordaining it was perfectly logical that Mr. Neale should be made an associate minister, called by the congregation, and ordained by them. Since Mr. Neale had refused to accept as much as $200 per month in salary, the trustees voted to fix his compensation at $150 per month until September, and from that time on at $1500 per year. Now Mr. Neale was being paid exactly the same salary as the first minister of the church, William Ware. This compared to Dr. Simon's salary of $9,000 per year.

At the congregational meeting on May 19, with 75 persons present, Mark Maclay reported that

> *Dr. Simons health was not improved, that Mr. Neale as acting minister under the board of trustees had shown a great deal of skill, and had managed to keep everything going, including funerals, Sunday services, etc. . . the only solution of the present situation, therefore, is having actively at the head of the church a person who is a duly ordained minister. There are two ways of reaching that result. One is to bring in from the outside an ordained minister and the other is to make one."(2)*

After explaining Unitarian and Congregational theory and practice about the ordination of ministers by a congregation, Mr. Maclay described this process as being consistent with the American theory of government. He also described to the congregation the difference between an assistant minister and an associate minister, for obviously some questions had been raised about this matter. He also explained that an associate minister is not a full minister; but is associated with another minister. He explained further that the church was not in a position to call another full time minister at the moment. The congregation did not want a temporary makeshift. He explained that there was no expectation on the part of anyone concerned that Mr. Neale's appointment in any way, directly or indirectly, implied that Mr. Neale was to be Dr. Simon's successor.

Mr. Maclay then went on to explain what was usually a very

sensitive point about ordaining a layman, and especially one who had almost no training for the ministry. The fellowship committee of the American Unitarian Association had made extended efforts to see to it that only persons qualified for the ministry were to be ordained as ministers. In Mr. Neale's case, he had previously had no reason to go before the fellowship committee.

Most young candidates met with this committee when they decided to seek a pulpit. Mr. Maclay suggested that if the congregation called Mr. Neale to be the associate minister, that his name would be submitted to a meeting of the fellowship committee which happened to be scheduled for the following morning, and that the congregation should leave further matters to the board of trustees who should act only if a certificate of fellowship were to be granted. In the motion which was then passed it was stated that Mr. Neale was not necessarily to be Dr. Simon's successor. A free expression of opinion was called for, and this followed.

All of the remarks about Mr. Neale were exceedingly affirmative as recorded in the minutes, and the proposition to make Laurance I. Neale the associate minister of All Souls Church was adopted unanimously by a rising vote. Dr. Simons, very close to death, wrote a letter to Dr. Frederick May Eliot, in which he praised Mr. Neale, stressed the necessity for a minister of the church who could function as a minister, and concluded: "And so I hope that the Fellowship Committee will see the justification of my suggestion that Laurance I. Neale be ordained and installed as associate minister of All Souls and that his application for fellowship be granted as soon as is reasonably possible."(3)

The fellowship committee of the American Unitarian Association met the next day in Boston, and granted Mr. Neale a provisional certificate of fellowship, which was the normal and usual procedure. Dr. Simons died five days later, and Mr. Neal became an associate minister with no one with whom to associate. But he was now in active charge of the church.

Mr. Neale became the Rev. Mr. Neale on Sunday afternoon, June 15, 1941, when a Service of Ordination and Installation was held in the church. Mr. Maclay as the president of the board of trustees acted as the spokesman for the congregation in the service. The sermon was given by Dr. Frederick May Eliot, who as the president of the American Unitarian Association was now a familiar figure to the members of All Souls. Mr. Neale, as is the custom, gave the Benediction.

Searching for Simons' Successor

The congregation now set out to find a new minister to re place Dr. Simons. A committee was appointed with Mr. Maclay and Mr. Neale as ex-officio members, and this committee began serious work in search of an adequate successor. The committee consisted of Dr. James M. Dunning, Mark Maclay, Rudolph Neuendorffer, Mrs. Anita L. Pearson, Miss Margaret Roys, and Charles Strong.

On November 5, 1941, Albert Williams, who had been the sexton of the church for many years, died. Mr. Neale described him thus: "It was Albert Williams' soul that endeared him to us much more than the hundred and one little tasks that he performed for us. . . . He knew sympathy, and gave of himself."(4) Mr. Williams had served as the sexton for twenty years and had been made a deacon in 1941. In those days sextons in New York churches often also served as the undertaker, and Mr. Albert Williams performed this duty at All Souls. A plaque was erected in his memory in the vestibule on May 24, 1942. Walter Williams, Albert's brother, was appointed funeral director.

The attack on Pearl Harbor came on December 7, 1941. But the impact of the war was not to come immediately to the All Souls congregation. It came later when the young men and women of the church began to leave the city to serve in the armed forces. There is mention in the minutes of air raid precautions, but this was the extent of the impact of the war for the moment.

Rafael Torres was now appointed building superintendent to succeed Albert Williams. He had been associated with the church as Albert Williams' assistant as early as 1929, and was to serve for many more years as the sexton. Mrs. Alfred J. Croft was appointed as church secretary, to serve in that capacity until the retirement of Dr. Neale in 1955.

The Choice of Neale

When the trustees met in January, 1942, the most important matter was a report from the president of the board of trustees, Mark W. Maclay, about the work of the committee to find a successor for Dr. Simons. They had wanted Dr. Frederick May Eliot to accept a call to the pulpit, but he told them that he was not available for consideration until the expiration of his present term as president of the American Unitarian Association. No other minister in the denomination appeared to satisfy all of the committee. The report stated:

The committee found that not only among its own members but also among the congregation generally, there was a very strong sentiment in favor of calling Mr. Neale as Dr. Simons successor. . . It was felt that he had demonstrated marked success in preaching, in the business conduct of the Church and the church office, in increasing attendance and interest, in grasp of financial problems, in development and stimulation of younger people, and in personal parish work.(5)

The president of the board therefore stated that the recommendation of the committee was that Mr. Neale be elected Dr. Simons successor, and that this matter be put to a vote of the congregation as soon as possible. The vote had been five to one in the committee. The dissenting vote of Mr. Charles H. Strong was based upon the ground that this job required a man of national prominence. Mr. Strong felt that it was too much to expect that a man could step so quickly into the pulpit of one of the most prominent Unitarian churches and continue to build up the church.

Since it was not possible to meet the required time set by the By-Laws, the annual meeting in 1942 could not act upon the matter. The matter was taken up at a special meeting called for February 2, 1942, with 86 voting members present. Mark Maclay spoke about the seriousness of the matter to come before the meeting. He said; "When Laurance Neale was called as associate minister of this church last May it was purely as associate, and for the purpose of keeping the ministry of this church going during an emergency."(6)

Mark Maclay then went on to outline the various things that had happened since that time. A committee had been appointed, all available sources for a minister had been canvassed, many of the ministers who had preached during these months "were not selected at random but for the very good purpose of giving the congregation a chance to hear them and to remember them."(7) But no one candidate had stood out with the exception of Dr. Eliot.

Mr. Maclay then gave a list of qualities for which they had looked in the various candidates; biographical material, where he was educated, etc., religious, cultural, and social point of view, personal convictions, denominational attitude, personality, conduct of public worship, ability to conduct parish duties, business ability, and last but not least preaching ability. The committee felt that in almost all of these qualities Mr. Neale ranked very high. "There may be many ministers in the denomination," Mr. Maclay continued, "but the committee could not possibly conceive of our finding out about them as we had already satisfied ourselves about Mr. Neale."(8)

Mr. Maclay then pointed out the other side of the picture. Mr. Neale had not had long training in the profession of the ministry. He explained that the headquarters at 25 Beacon Street in Boston was very doubtful about this experiment, and particularly about such a precedent in so large a church in the denomination. Mr. Neale had had almost no theological training. Mark Maclay also said; "It is quite understandable that headquarters feels that we are letting them down in going counter to their views by placing in command of this parish a man who has held a union ticket, so to say, only a short time."(9)

But Mr. Maclay felt that this was a particularly proper exception to the rules of the association. Charles Strong was ill and was not able to be present at the meeting. So Mark Maclay presented Mr. Strong's view that no man could suddenly step into such ministerial responsibility. Mr. Strong believed in keeping Mr. Neale's services as associate minister if not as minister. Mr. Maclay read letters from Francis Rogers, and Frederick W. Ecker who were unable to be present, expressing approval. Rudolph Neuendorffer then spoke to the meeting about the time element and Mr. Neale's knowledge of business affairs which would be important in the coming years of the church. He also expressed his opinion that it was not against Unitarian principles to call one of their own people to be their minister. He then moved to call Laurance I. Neale, and that he be paid a salary of $3500 per year plus $2500 for parsonage expenses. Miss Margaret Roys and Dr. James W. Dunning spoke favorably, as did Mr. Blaney. Dr. Foot asked about the attitude of headquarters, and Mr. Maclay explained that the congregation had not called Mr. Neale with any specific idea that he would succeed Dr. Simons. Headquarters had understood this to mean that Mr. Neale would not be called as Dr. Simons' successor. Mr. Maclay inferred that the misunderstanding with head quarters could have been due to the fact that the committee did not inform headquarters of the change in their thinking.

The debate continued. Francis White, who termed himself a "young person," felt that perhaps the committee was acting too hurriedly. There were more speeches and some letters were read. Mark Maclay even left the chair and made a speech. He believed that the church was not working in opposition to the denomination's attempts to build up a well-qualified ministry by "recognizing a proper exception to it." He then returned to the chair and spoke about the right of a minority. He did not feel that the vote would be unanimous, and he did not want it to be so. It was also voted that votes in letters in the hands of the chairman be counted in the balloting. This was in opposition to the By-Laws of the church which allowed no votes by proxy. Mrs. L. Lawrence White asked that a transcription of the minutes of the meeting be sent to Dr. Eliot, a motion which was carried.

The tellers then announced the count. The ballot showed 81

in the affirmative, no negative votes, and no blank votes. Of the eight votes cast by proxy (letters), 7 were affirmative and 2 were negative.(lO) Since all the qualified voters present had voted to call Mr. Neale, it was moved to make the vote unanimous, and this motion was carried. At the close of the meeting Joseph W. Drake, a prominent lawyer, said that the congregation must realize the seriousness of what they had done, that they had called Mr. Neale in disregard of the expressed opinion of headquarters, and for that reason Mr. Neale needed heartfelt support from all of the people in his work from now on. He said; "If we do not support him, we leave him out on a limb."(11) In spite of all of the speeches, the meeting only took two and one half hours.

But those hours were to prove very significant in the relation ship of All Souls with the Unitarian denomination. Although everything on the surface appeared to have been healed, the words of Joseph Drake were prophetic in that the church which at one time was ready to call the president of the American Unitarian Association as their minister, had now aroused his opposition in the matter by calling a layman. Dr. Eliot told me several times about this event, and Mark Maclay stated it properly when he said that All Souls had indicated that they had not any idea at the time Mr. Neale was associate minister that he would ever be called as the minister.

It was somewhat ironic that in 1958 Dr. Eliot was to die of a heart attack at the gate to Memorial Garden having given the last sermon of his life the day before to a congregation which had welcomed him as the only suitable candidate to their pulpit, and then when he had refused, and they had selected another, of whose qualifications Dr. Eliot did not approve, that there should have been strained relations. From that time on the church was considered something of an outcast by many in the denomination, and although both Neale and Eliot tried to smooth things over, very little was done for many years to change the situation.

Dealing With the Debt

Two new memorials were added to those already in the church, a plaque commemorating the services of Minot Simons in the sanctuary, and a plaque in the vestibule commemorating the services of Albert Williams. Otto Langmann, an architect who was a member of All Souls, donated his services in designing the memorials, and they were unveiled together on Sunday May 24, 1942.

On October 11, 1942, William H. Brewster was appointed as organist at a salary of $2500 per annum. Mr. Brewster served the church in this capacity until 1967, twenty-five years.

It was reported that in the year 1942 fifty persons had signed the membership book. This indicated that the church was on an upward swing, and that the decision to move the church building to a new neighborhood had been a wise choice. Prior to this year the average number of members joining each year had been about 30. There were also 22 marriages at All Souls during that year, many of them being what were called "war marriages." Mark Maclay announced at the annual meeting in 1943 that 59 men from All Souls families were now in the armed services of the nation, and to show how the church congregation changed over the years, I have known in my ministry, which began ten years after the war ended, only eight of these men.

Mr. Maclay was also able to report that the Franklin Savings Bank had further reduced the rate of interest to one-and-one-half percent a year, and the amortization to one percent. Two hundred and nineteen persons had subscribed to the Every Member Canvass during 1942, and Mr. Neale's salary was increased to $4,000, plus his parsonage allowance. In 1943, the sum realized from the Every Member Canvass was $17,190, from 270 subscribers. There were 92 children in the church Sunday school. Miss Reed left to become the director of religious education in the Presbyterian church of South Orange, New Jersey. Miss Elizabeth Bright McKinney was chosen to succeed her.

In January 1945, the congregation assembled for their usual

annual meeting. This meeting, however, was somewhat unusual because the debt problem had reached a point of crisis. In his annual report Mr. Maclay mentioned that the debt on the church held by the Franklin Savings Bank now stood at $355,640. The arrangement to pay one-and-one-half-percent interest and to amortize at one percent had expired as it was a three-year agreement. The board had hoped to present a concrete proposal at this meeting, but circumstances had made this impossible. Mark Maclay stated that the mortgage was now simply an overdue mortgage upon which the bank could foreclose if they so desired. Mr. Maclay assured the congregation; "I do not think that they will, but it is their right."(12) He warned the people that sometime during 1945 it was going to be necessary to raise a lot of money. This report did not come as a surprise to the congregation; they knew that financially the church had been living on borrowed time.

At the meeting of the trustees in April, 1945, it was reported that after a conference with the Franklin Savings Bank, Frederick W. Ecker, acting for the church, had made an offer of $180,000 to retire the mortgage of $355,640. The bank had refused this offer, but had made a counter-offer of $250,000 to settle the matter. A congregational meeting was set for April 19th to discuss the bank's offer. Mr. Neale was to go over the list of possible prospects for gifts, and the Baker Estate trustees were to be contacted immediately in hopes that the estate might be willing to match dollar for dollar what the congregation raised. A "Burn the Mortgage Campaign" was ready to be put into motion.

This account, which is taken from the official records, is far less dramatic than the story that is commonly told about how Miss Margaret Roys, after a trustees meeting, went home, and said to her room-mate, Miss Goodale, that she would give $1,000 that she had saved for a rainy day if others would do the same. Her housemate, Miss Goodale, agreed with her, and promised to match the gift. Frederick W. Ecker was authorized to approach the Franklin Savings Bank to tell them that the trustees proposed to raise the $250,000 by October 1, 1945, as a full settlement of the mortgage. Mr. Ward of the bank replied to Mr.

Ecker on April 18, 1945; "Please be advised that we are willing to accept the sum of $250,000 in full payment of the principal of the mortgage."(13) The die had been cast, and a campaign must be conducted to raise this amount, and very quickly. At the same time, Frederick Ecker and Mark Maclay came to an agreement with Percy Gardner, the treasurer of the American Unitarian Association, to borrow up to $125,000 against the pledges which the church hoped to have soon, but not all of them in cash. The fact that the denomination was so willing to help in many ways smoothed over the ruffled feelings between headquarters and the members of All Souls.

The special meeting of the society was held on April 19, 1945. The board presented its plan for raising the money before October 1, and Mr. Maclay made a case for the necessity to pay off the entire mortgage. Some evidently thought that it would be easier to raise a partial sum, but Mark Maclay pointed out that by accepting the banks' offer the church would save the sum of $105,640, not an inconsiderable sum of money. Then Mark Maclay told the story of Miss Roys. He read the letter which Miss Margaret Roys had written to him some months previously, and Mr. Maclay announced that they had $2,000 to start the campaign from these two dedicated women.

Frederick W. Ecker then spoke about the advantages from a business point of view. Mr. Ecker was the president of the Metropolitan Life Insurance Co. He pointed out that not only was the Franklin Savings Bank willing to assist the congregation, but that the United States government would also assist because of the present income tax law. He pointed out that it really cost a lot less to make a sizable gift than appeared on the surface because of the allowable charitable deduction. Laurance Neale gave a strong affirmation of the rightness of the project. Both Rudolph Neuendorffer and Elliott Benedict, the senior statesmen of the church, wrote strong letters of support. The motion was put to Mark Maclay who put the vote. It was unanimous!

Then Mark Maclay said:

This is April 19th. On April 18th Paul Revere rode, and sounded the alarm that the British were coming. And Paul Revere's ride was of no more significance to this country and the nation which was born, than the ride we start to-night at this church and the religious life of the city, and to the cause of Unitarianism in general. Churches are not built upon material things, but sometimes money must be necessary to save a human institution from dying.(14)

All Souls Church was a case in point.

The "Burn the Mortgage" Campaign

The campaign began. Twenty-eight persons worked on the assignment of names to be canvassed for the campaign. By June 2, there were 165 subscriptions for a total of $112,961, 21 of which were $1,000 subscriptions. Mark Maclay also told the trustees that the Baker Trust had agreed to pay the last $50,000 if the congregation raised $200,000. By September 21, foundations had been approached, with no results; but the campaign had reached a total of $168,335 from 342 contributors, with cash in the bank of $114,755. Margaret Roys would have received this word with welcome ears, but she was unable to attend the board meeting because of an accident, and the board sent her a word of sympathy.

A special meeting of the society was held on September 25. By this time the total contributed was $174,000, plus the Baker Trust gift. Mr. Maclay expressed the hope that before noon on Monday they would make the goal of the campaign. Somehow the money was raised. The "prospects" who had not come through, did come through. The debt was paid. The church was saved. The sum of $250,000 was paid to the Franklin Savings Bank on October 5, 1945, and they must have been glad to see the end of that loan. The amount that had been raised through future pledges was less than $50,000, and this amount had been borrowed from the American Unitarian Association, and a few days thereafter the account was brought down to $37,000. A great celebration was held in Fellowship Hall on October18, 1945, to celebrate the victory. Mark Maclay opened the meeting by thanking all of the people who had been responsible for the successful conclusion of the "Burn the Mortgage Campaign." Originally, he said, a list of about 450 names had been drawn up of people who might appropriately be solicited. This had been done by thirty volunteers. He particularly thanked Philip Lukin, an advertising executive and member of the church, who had written all of the publicity materials used in the campaign.

Mark Maclay then introduced Frederick W. Ecker, the president of the Metropolitan Life Insurance Co, and treasurer of the church. Mr. Ecker told the story of the negotiations with the Franklin Savings Bank that had led to the bank's offer to settle the debt. He announced that $251,798.42 had been raised to date. He thanked the American Unitarian Association for the loan of $50,000 as an advance on pledges already secured but not paid in full as yet. He also explained that although usually the expenses of a campaign such as this were high, that because so much talent had been donated, the entire cost of the campaign had been $1,132.42, mostly for printing.

Margaret Roys, the person who had sparked the campaign, then spoke. The hymn "Burn the Mortgage" was sung, and while it was being sung, Miss Roys was escorted to the stage of Fellowship Hall by Messrs. Neale, Maclay, Ecker, and Lukin. The other members of the committee went to the rear of Fellowship Hall; Benedict, Blaney, Corney, Dunning, Neuendorffer, Stanton, and Strong. Mrs. Francis Rogers could not be present. While the last chorus was being sung, Elliott Benedict bearing a copy of the mortgage on a pole, accompanied by the other five members of the committee, marched down the center aisle and on to the stage. Mr. Benedict placed the copy of the mortgage on top of a panel which had indicated the progress of the campaign while it was being conducted. Dr. Dunning manned a fire extinguisher, and the flame was lighted by Miss Roys, who announced that "the matches had been contributed by the Franklin Savings Bank." To conclude the meeting, Laurance Neale talked about the future opportunities of the church, especially in making Unitarianism better known in this great city.(15)

The War Years

During the war activities at the church were of necessity cur tailed. The celebration of the 125th Anniversary in 1944, was called: "A Service of Commemoration and Consecration." Even the Act of Consecration had overtones of the struggle of the war through which all were personally going. Mr. Neale led the congregation in the Act of Consecration.

With the vision fresh in our minds of those gallant souls who through a century and a quarter labored that others might live and have life and have it more abundantly, and with the consciousness of our own dear men who have fallen for their country, and those others who are now girded about the earth in endless fields of battle, we consecrate ourselves anew to spare no effort to create a world worthy of their sacrifices."(16)

At this service, Laurance Neale preached the sermon, Rudolph Neuendorffer led the congregation in the Bond of Union, Mark Maclay read the responsive reading, and Charles H. Strong gave an address of historical perspective called "As I Knew Them." The service concluded with the serving of communion by the deacons. The day had been designated as World Order Day by the Federal Council of Churches, and although Unitarians could not belong to this Protestant organization because of its creedal basis, Mr. Neale attempted to put together a service in memory, and one of looking forward to a better world.(17)

Just as the "Burn the Mortgage Campaign" spelled victory for the church, so also the world had seen the end of World War II. The Church was open on V-J Day on August 13, 14, and 15 from

8 A.M. to 10 P.M. so that people might go into the church and give thanks for the end of four years of war fought by America, and the end of six years of war in Europe.

A total of 140 members of All Souls families served in the armed forces during the war. Four men from All Souls gave their lives, and their sacrifice is commemorated in a series of photographs on the Mezzanine floor of the Church. Frazier Curtis was killed in an airplane accident in which he ordered his passengers to use their parachutes while he flew the plane. He waited too long to jump himself, and his parachute did not open. Jacques Rodney Eisner was killed on the bridge of the cruiser "U.S.S. San Francisco" in the Battle of the Solomon Islands. James Freeman Curtis was also killed in an airplane accident very similar to that in which his brother Frazier was killed. Adolph Paul Constantin Schramm Jr. died of disease contracted in line of duty.(18)

A prominent layman of the church who had died during the war was Hendrich Willem van Loon, who had signed the membership book in 1942, and gave the Layman's Sunday sermon that year on "History and Leadership." Dr. van Loon was noted as a popular writer and geographer who had written many books. Mr. Neale conducted the funeral service in March, 1944.

Mr. Neale also conducted the funeral of a famous musician in 1945. Bela Bartok had fled his native Hungary in 1940. Bartok was something of a freethinker in matters of religion in Hungary where Unitarianism is strong. He had come to New York in poor health, had lectured at Columbia University for a while, but then almost everyone lost track of him, and he lived in poverty in the city. He was desperately ill, and consented to go to the hospital only when he realized that it might be the only thing that would save him. When he died, although he was not a member of All Souls, his friends thought that the Unitarian church was the clos est to his religious convictions. Mr. Neale conducted the funeral which took place at the Universal Funeral Chapel on September 28, 1945. Bartok was buried in Woodlawn Cemetery, and in 1988 his remains were moved back to his native Hungary where he is now a famous man and a national hero. His son, Bela Bartok, Jr.

carried out his father's wishes by this act. The younger Bartok has acted as the lay president of the Unitarians in Hungary.

The Post-War Years

At the end of 1946, Philip Lukin, an advertising executive, and chairman of the committee on membership, attendance, and public relations, reported to the trustees on the results of a survey which the committee had completed under Mr. Lukin's guidance. What the survey showed was that in spite of doubts about Mr. Neale's ability to attract new members to the church, the number joining the church had rapidly increased. By the time the survey was taken in 1946, 22% of the membership had joined since Mr. Neale had become the minister. The committee also discovered that the average commuting time to church was half an hour. It is interesting to note that the critics of various aspects of the church program were much better attenders than the non-critics. Perhaps they knew more things about which to be critical than the non-attenders.

The conclusions of the survey were summarized in these words:

The Church is now in a very vital condition. Attendance at services has increased, and activities are likewise increasing in all functions. Similarly the membership is increasing. The report also concluded that the Church was under-staffed, and that the attendance which had averaged 112 persons a Sunday for the ten years from 1932-1941, was definitely on the increase, attendance now being in the neighborhood of an average of 125-130.(19)

Mark Maclay reported to the board on January 6, 1947, that Mr. Neale had undergone an operation for a cataract in one eye on the day after Christmas, "the operation seemed to be a success, but that the results would not be known until the time for fitting glasses." He said that "Mr. Neale was very restive, which surprised no one, that he talked on the telephone once a day with Mrs. Croft at the church office, and that he hoped to be discharged from the hospital the end of the week.(20)

In order to make the Unitarian message better known, through the help of C. Chester Lane, who was the assistant business manager of the *New York Times,* a contract had been signed with Radio Station WQXR, the Times station, for programs to run for thirteen weeks on Sunday afternoons at 3:30 P.M. They were to be delivered by Mr. Neale, and they were to be titled, "A Liberal Minister Looks At Life." The cost of the thirteen programs was about $3,000. A second series was later authorized by the trustees.

There were some problems with the building. It was not the roof trouble which had plagued the former church buildings. It was steeple trouble. Otto Langmann, who had been the associate architect when the church was built, wrote to the trustees on April 14, 1948, that the mortar in the joints of the Texas limestone cornices and copings had disintegrated, and that it was imperative to rake out the old mortar, and to fill the crevices with a mastic waterproof compound topped with a lead covering. The cost was estimated at $4,200. The work would have to be done by a steeple jack on a swing tied to the top of the steeple. At that time steeple-jacks earned $3.50 per hour. The work was completed, and every fifteen or twenty years since that time has had to be done again.

Frederick W. Ecker, the president of the board of trustees, announced at the annual meeting in 1947, that for the first time a balanced budget was being presented; thanks, he said, to the success of the "Burn the Mortgage Campaign." Mr. Ecker in deference to his father, also with the same name, and who had preceded him as president of the Metropolitan Life Insurance Co., who was an ardent Episcopalian, never actually joined All Souls Church. Yet he was very active in the church, and his membership was only a technicality.

In January 1947, Raphael Torres was appointed sexton of the church. He had worked at All Souls as early as 1919 at the first parish supper cooked for a repast prior to the annual meeting by Mrs. Laurence Sullivan. He had worked full time at the church since 1929 as an assistant to Albert Williams. Now he was appointed the sexton, and since by this time professional undertakers had taken over the job formerly assigned to the sexton, he no longer served as undertaker.

On May 25, 1947, a tablet to George F. Baker (1840-1931) and to his son, George F. Baker (1878-1937) was dedicated. It is located on the north wall of the sanctuary. We have already spoken at length of the help of the Bakers at a very critical time in the life of the Church. The Bakers were very generous in their giving to various institutions, and the Stadium at Columbia University, the library at Dartmouth College, and the original buildings of the Business School at Harvard were evidences of their generosity. Just to show that George F. Baker (the elder Baker) had an ecumenical spirit, he contributed a million dollars toward the building of the Cathedral of Saint John the Divine in New York City.

At the annual meeting held on January 18, 1949, Mr. Neale told the congregation about a controversy that had taken place during the past year. He had been invited to take part in a traditional Neighborhood Vesper Service planned by the private schools in the city which took place that year at St. James Episcopal Church. Bishop Manning of the Episcopal Diocese of New York had written a letter to the *New York Herald Tribune* complaining about Mr. Neale's presence in the service, on the ground that since the church was founded upon the Apostle's Creed, and that since Mr. Neale disagreed with the validity of that creed, that Mr. Neale should have had no part in the service.

The press had besieged Mr. Neale to make some comment, but he was loathe to make an issue of the Bishop's letter. But he did say that "In a world which needed so much to find unity in diversity, it was a pity to insist upon conformity, and that it was equally a pity to introduce dogma about Jesus when what is needed is adherence to his spirit."(21) On the following Sunday morning, just before he began his sermon, Dr. Kinsolving, the rector of St. James Church, told his congregation how much he regretted the letter of Bishop Manning, that he did not agree with the Bishop at all, and that he stood squarely behind the interdenominational services. Dr. Kinsolving had given Mr. Neale his own personal apology for the incident, and Dr. Hugh McCandless of the Church of the Epiphany also expressed his personal regrets.

The death of Charles Howard Strong at his summer home "Stronghold" at Roque Bluff, Maine, on July 29, 1949, removed from All Souls ranks one of its most distinguished twentieth century members. He had been active for fifty-nine years in the affairs of the church. For many of these years he was a trustee. From 1919 to 1921 he was the president of the board of trustees, and at the time of his death was serving as senior deacon.

Mr. Strong had been born on October 6, 1865 in Jerseyville, Illinois, the son of John Caldwell Strong and Mary Cornelia Butcher Strong. After graduating from Harvard in 1887, he took his law degree there in 1890. He came to New York City and immediately established himself as an important person at the New York bar. In 1922, Harvard conferred upon him the honorary degree of Master of Arts. He served as the first president of the national organization of the Unitarian Laymen's League. For many years he was the chairman of the Board of Trustees of the Meadville Theological School in Chicago. He served on the Board of Directors and the Executive Committee of the Greater New York Federation of Churches. He played a conspicuous role, along with Clarence Darrow, in the "Scopes Trial" at Dayton, Tennessee. He helped defend school teacher John T. Scopes who was teaching the theory of evolution in Tennessee schools.

After the First World War he served as vice-president and chairman of the board of directors of the American Association for the League of Nations. He was president of the City Club from 1909 until 1914. He was secretary of the Association of the Bar of the City of New York from 1917 until 1946. He served on many other civic and cultural boards. Judge Frederick Longfellow Strong, a retired New York City judge, still active at All Souls, is his son.(22)

Building Wiggin House

At the meeting of the trustees on November 20, 1951, Mr. Neale was able to report that a long cherished hope was about to be realized. Mrs. Albert Henry Wiggin had offered to give the church a sum of up to $300,000 for the creation of a parish house and chapel as a memorial to her husband, the late Albert Henry Wiggin, long a member of the church, and a member of the board of trustees. He had also served on the investment commit tee. One of the reasons that Mrs. Wiggin made this gift was that the Chase National Bank, of which Mr. Wiggin had been the president, was merging with the Manhattan Bank, and in the merger process Mrs. Wiggin's stock had acquired a new value. In her generosity she shared her good fortune with the church.

I had heard that Albert Henry Wiggin was the son of a Unitarian minister, so I looked up his father, and discovered to my great surprise some astonishing things about the elder Wiggin's life. James Henry Wiggin (1836-1900) was a Unitarian clergyman. He graduated from Tufts College and Meadville Theological School. He held various pastorates in Unitarian churches in Massachusetts. In 1875 he moved to New York City to edit *The Liberal Christian,* a Unitarian publication. But he never felt comfortable away from Boston. He supplied a few pulpits, but he was more interested in writing. In 1885 he was asked by Mary Baker Eddy to assist in the preparation of the 16th edition of *Science and Health.* He revised the whole book, much simplifying the style of Mrs. Eddy. He also assisted in later editions. In 1891 Mrs. Eddy accused him of being under the influence of "Malicious Animal Magnetism," and the relationship ended. So a Unitarian clergy man actually edited and possibly rewrote a great deal of Mrs. Eddy's very influential book in the history of American religion.(23)

In view of Mrs. Wiggin's gift, the trustees agreed to try to raise $100,000 among the members to increase the general endowment funds. There would be increased expenses for the up keep of Wiggin House. The drive was under way by October.

The groundbreaking ceremony took place following the

morning service on October 12, 1952. The congregation repaired to the garden next door, and Mrs. Jessie Duncan Hayden Wiggin turned the first spadeful of earth for the new Wiggin House. The address on the occasion was given by C. Chester Lane, the presi dent of the board of trustees. In November, the trustees published a booklet called The Wiggin House Fund For a Greater All Souls, which described the new building and what it would mean for the church's future. On Wednesday, July 22, 1953, the cornerstone of Wiggin House was laid in a simple ceremony in which the minis ter, the officers, the architects, the builders, and a few church members were present. Some papers were put in a copper box and then into the cornerstone. Mr. Neale concluded the services with a brief prayer. In the box were pictures of Mr. and Mrs. Wiggin, some articles about the life of Mr. Wiggin, a few pamphlets about the church, and appropriate sermons by Dr. Simons and Mr. Neale. By December, the amount raised for the fund amounted only to a total of $28,451. The church was having trouble rais ing capital funds so closely upon the conclusion of the "Burn the Mortgage Campaign" of 1945 in which members had stretched their resources in order to make it a success. By the end of the year the fund had raised the sum of $77,249 which included several large gifts from Mrs. Wiggin.

The dedication of Wiggin House took place on Easter Sun day afternoon, April 18, 1954, construction having been delayed by a strike in the building trades, and other unavoidable events. Dr. Eliot brought greetings from the Unitarian churches. Mr. C. Chester Lane gave the address, and the builder, Charles Herman Tyler gave the keys to Mrs. Wiggin, and they were accepted by Mr. Lane. Mr. Lane called attention to the fact that Albert Wig gin had been the son of a Unitarian minister, and that Mr. Wiggin "learned in a simple Massachusetts parsonage the basic principles of service and thrift and faith, which made him a commanding figure in New York City and the nation." Reviewing Mr. Wiggin's life, Chester Lane illustrated the constant challenges that he had from his simple New England home to that of president of one of the world's greatest banks. His thanks to Mrs. Wiggin for the new

Parish House were shared by all those present.(24)

The Memorial Garden

On October 12, 1953, Mr. and Mrs. Samuel H. Ordway made a gift of $12,000, with a contribution of the same amount to be given the following year, to build a garden at All Souls in memory of two of their children who had died, Anna Hanson Ordway and Stephen Wheatland Ordway. "If a garden was acceptable to all concerned. . . our idea would be to have it look like a home gar den and not a show place," they wrote to Mr. Neale.(25) The board accepted this wonderful gift which provided not only for the establishment of the Memorial Garden but also for its upkeep from year to year. The Ordways had been very prominent nationally in the movement to preserve unusual lands for future generations and this garden on Lexington Avenue when stumbled upon by visitors, comes as a great and pleasant surprise to those who think of New York City as everything paved over with cement or blacktop.

The author was extremely fortunate to be present for the dedication of the Memorial Garden, for I was the guest preacher at All Souls that morning. I preached on the subject "A Man's Own Religion." Dr. Neale had a Christening service that morning, and as I saw the little baby brought down the aisle by her proud parents, I wondered as a stranger to New York City whether there was a place for a little baby in the midst of all of this concrete. Mr. Neale did not understand what I was talking about, a man raised in a small California town, for this was home to him. I later understood that little babies have a real place in such a city. That afternoon when I looked at the newly planted and landscaped garden I realized that the Ordways had presented to the church a bit of God's nature. All Souls has the garden because the Ordways were interested seriously in the conservation of natural resources all over the nation. Why not start in their home city, New York City, with a bit of nature?

A Surprise Retirement

At the annual meeting of the society held on January 18, 1955, Mr. Neale concluded his annual report with a surprise announcement:

As I look into the future I see that on the 20th day of next July I shall be 70 years old. I am therefore telling you that it is my intention to retire from the active ministry of this church on the first of September of this year.

It is very important that you have a younger man to carry on. The first two ministers of All Souls, William Ware and Henry W. Bellows, were both 24 years old when they stepped into the ministry here; and the last two ministers, Dr. Simons, my predecessor, and I, both of us, were fifty-five years old when we began our ministries. That shows a tendency of our time. It may be desirable to reverse the tendency at least to give serious thought to the introduction of younger people.

It has been a wonderful fifteen years for me. I have been blessed by health. For two months in '47 I could not attend to my duties because of an operation for the removal of a cataract from one of my eyes, but with that exception, through this whole period of my ministry I have never missed a service or any other stated engagement requiring my presence. The Lord has been good to me, and he has blessed my two girls too (Mrs. Neale, and his sister Miss Neale) without whom I could not do anything. It is just myself about whom I am talking tonight. It is about you and a good many others who are not here. who by putting their shoulders to the wheel made possible whatever success we have achieved. I want to help you as much as I may in the future; but it is important that I relinquish the responsibility of directing the life of the church.

There is one thing that I should like to do before I die, and that is to write a history of All Souls; but the active ministry of this church should be placed in the hands of a younger, more vigorous man, a man who can see things as he looks

The Original Wiggin House (Architect's Drawing)

The Wiggin House Chapel. Photo: George E. Joseph.

ahead, that perhaps my eyes are too dim to perceive. I am grateful for all you have done to help me. You will always be my dear friends.(26)

This announcement took everyone by surprise including the trustees. C. Chester Lane, as chairman of the meeting, felt that the whole matter should be discussed at a later meeting when it could be treated adequately. Mark Maclay felt that he could not resist saying something about Mr. Neale's service to the church, and that the congregation should abide by Mr. Neale's wishes.

I can think of nothing more appropriate than Larry Neale writing a history of this church which he knows better than anyone else, and to do it while he is in full possession of his faculties. . . I think that we all ought to think it over.(27)

On this note the meeting adjourned.

On Sunday afternoon, June 12th, at the Ninety-Ninth Commencement of Tufts University, Mr. Neale was awarded the degree of Doctor of Divinity (D.D.) and became Dr. Neale. President Nils Y. Wessel, made the following citation in part;

Successful business man who turned his talents to man's spiritual needs, you embody the high ideals and deep concern for the welfare of fellow men which might well motivate all of us."(28)

The resignation of Mr. Neale, now Dr. Neale, brought an end to a very difficult era in the history of All Souls. A man who was deemed to be untrained for the position by a denominational leader, proved that the ministry and the business of running a large metropolitan church is essentially one of administration and inspiration through preaching. Dr. Neale had accomplished what few ministers do in their careers. He had moved into a most demanding profession far different than the profession for which he was educated and in which he had experience, and by devoted and

The Memorial Garden. The Enlarged Wiggin House can be seen in the background. Photo: George E. Joseph.

diligent pursuit of the best that he could do, proved to be the right man, in the right place, at the right time.

Dr. Neale became ill shortly after the first of January, 1956, after his retirement in September. He was slated to be the preacher for the Memorial Service for the 50th anniversary of his class at Harvard College. He was ill during all of the winter months, and passed away at Mid-town Hospital on Easter eve, March 31, 1956. Perhaps he knew something that no one else knew when he surprised the congregation with his resignation just a little more than a year prior to his death.

He was never to write his precious history of All Souls.

The church calendar for April 8, had a page devoted to his life, and expressed the sentiments of the congregation.

Dr. Neale was a man of high principles, unostentatious, and dedicated to the cause of liberal religion in the City of New York. .He was a bulwark in time of trouble. . . He set an example in this church and community for which he will long be remembered." The passage from Luke sounds strangely familiar, "Did not our hearts burn within us while he talked with us."(29)

The members of the congregation erected a tablet on the south wall of the sanctuary to honor him and his ministry. A library in his memory was also established in the Ware Room by a grateful congregation.

Walter Donald Kring. Eighth Minister of All Souls 1955-1978. The ceramic jar in the foreground is the work of the famous British potter Bernard Leach.

CHAPTER 6

A Potter Shapes The Church:

The Ministry of Walter Donald Kring (1955-1978)

> *Religion is not superstition. Religion is the attempt to find the fundamental meaning of existence. . . judging everything that we do and know critically, seeking to find the unknown not only in the realm of science and mathematics, but also in the realm of man's relationship to man and man's relationship to what we call the spiritual factors of existence. To be religious a person must constantly be asking himself such a question as this, "What is the fundamental meaning of life? (1)*
>
> Walter Donald Kring

Again All Souls Church faced what had appeared to be one of its most difficult problems, finding a minister to the liking of the congregation. Mr. Neale had suggested that the new minister ought to be a young man since both he and Dr. Simons were fifty-five years of age when they began their ministry. So at their meeting on January 25, 1955, the board of trustees appointed a search committee composed of C. Chester Lane, chairman, Raymond S. Fanning, Samuel M. Lane, Mark W. Maclay, Mrs. Kenneth Miller, Mrs. Abner Raeburn, with Mr. Neale as ex-officio. On February 15, the board of trustees heard the names of the ministers who were being considered. The committee had

145

made arrangements for several of its members to go to the home churches of these ministers to hear them preach.

An Unorthodox Search

The search committee heard these ministers in their own pulpits, and then had Mr. Neale make arrangements for six of them to preach during the spring at All Souls. The church was not following the recommended procedure which was for the committee to choose a single candidate. But it was also a strange procedure be cause none of the candidates knew that he was being considered. Having a series of ministers preach at All Souls when the congregation knew they were candidates and the candidates themselves did not know was an unorthodox procedure. The candidates made no application for the position. They were not told by Mr. Neale that there was any candidating going on.

On February 6, 1955, Rev. Arthur Foote, minister of the Unity Church in Saint Paul, Minnesota, was the preacher. He was the successor to Dr. Frederick May Eliot in that pulpit. Dr. Bradford Eugene Gale, minister of the First Church (Unitarian) in Salem, Massachusetts, preached on February 20. Rev. Walter Donald Kring, minister of the First Unitarian Church in Worcester, Massachusetts, was the guest preacher on April 24. Rev. Waldemar W. Argow Jr., minister of the Peoples Church of Cedar Rapids, Iowa, was the preacher on May 1. On May 15, Rev. Carl Bihldorff, minister of the First Parish in Brookline, Massachusetts, was the preacher. On May 22, Rev. Richard M. Steiner, minister of the Unitarian Church of Our Father, in Portland Oregon, was the preacher.

Since there was no acknowledged candidating procedure, and since none of the men knew for certain that they were candidates, it is difficult to know which of these ministers were actually candidates. The congregation now had had a chance to hear the ministers whom the search committee believed were possible candidates for the pulpit. Undoubtedly, in an informal manner, the members of the committee heard the comments of the parishioners.

A Candidate Proposed

On May 17, Chester Lane reported to the board of trustees that the committee "after careful investigation, and after listening in their own churches to a number of candidates, had decided to recommend Rev. Walter Donald Kring, minister of the First Unitarian Church of Worcester, Massachusetts, as the man best suited for the position of minister to succeed Mr. Neale.(2)

Since it had to be ascertained "Whether Mr. Kring would accept the call of the Church," Mr. Lane suggest the appointment of a small committee to discuss this matter with Mr. Kring, and to make financial arrangements if he were to be the candidate. Chester Lane and Mark Maclay were to discuss this matter with Mr. Kring, and the conditions under which he would. accept the position of minister. It was also decided to call a special meeting of the Congregation on Wednesday, June 8.

At this special meeting, Mr. Lane suggested that the first order of business was a sad one, the acceptance of the resignation of Dr. Laurance I. Neale which he had made at the annual meeting in January. Such a motion making Mr. Neale's resignation effective as of September 1, was passed with deep regret.

The next step, said Mr. Lane, was a happy one, to report the work of the search committee to choose a new minister. He spoke about a suggested a list of qualifications that had been used the same list that had been used when Mr. Neale was selected. The committee had tried to hear each minister in his own church and then the ministers had been invited to preach at All Souls. The committee had decided to make a single recommendation. The committee did not agree with the suggestion that all of these men be brought again as candidates to All Souls to preach.

Although we realized that we were endangering any unanimous decision. . . we felt that as a democratic procedure we should let the congregation hear as many of these persons as seemed to us might be worth considering.(3)

At this point in the meeting, after a brief biographical summary of the candidate's life, the motion was made that the nomminations be closed. It was suggested that a unanimous vote ought to be made. Samuel M. Lane said, "Why not bring him in with our arms wide open, saying that we all want him, and that none of us feels reluctant in the choice."(4) Someone asked if Mr. Kring's availability had been ascertained, and Chester Lane replied that had. The secretary was asked to cast a single ballot for him. A salary was then voted after Mr. Lane explained that the most ministers in the denomination in large churches were receiving far more than All Souls had paid in the past, because Mr. Neale had private income. The final action of the meeting was to make Rev. Laurance I. Neale, minister emeritus with a salary of $3,600 per year.

The Eighth Minister

The church calendar for Sunday June 19, had a picture of the new minister, and a summary of his career. The fall schedule began on Sunday September 18, 1955, when Mr. Kring gave his first sermon as the eighth minister of All Souls. In the pastoral letter which appeared in the church calendar, Mr. Kring said something about his concept of the ministry in a Unitarian Church.

I believe in absolute honesty in the conduct of the ministry. . . I also believe that we do not all have to think exactly alike in or der to worship together. . . I conceive of the church as an institution that requires a particular kind of loyalty. We shall accomplish our potential only if we shall all work together in the spirit of the religion which we profess.(5)

Just who was this new minister that All Souls apparently had chosen so easily compared to what had been such a difficult process in times past?(6)

Walter Donald Kring was born at 1566 Warren Road in Lakewood, Ohio on March 10, 1916. A younger brother, Robert, who died in 1963, was born on May 13, 1920. The family moved to Columbus, Ohio, in 1923, and Mr. Kring took a position as director of religious education at the Broad Street Presbyterian Church in Columbus. In 1929 he was asked to consider a similar position in Santa Ana, California. He packed the family off to Santa Ana just in time to face the Great Depression. Walter Donald graduated from Santa Ana High School in 1933. The family went through the Long Beach earthquake on March 10, 1933 (Walter's 17th birthday). It was the second worst earthquake in modern times, next to the San Francisco earthquake of 1906 in destructive power.

Southern California had an excellent Junior College system, so Walter attended Santa Ana Junior College his Freshman year. In 1934 the family moved to Pasadena, California, where Mr. Kring had been fortunate to obtain a position as director of religious education at the Westminster Presbyterian Church in Altadena, a suburb of Pasadena. Quite naturally, Walter Donald went to Occidental College for his Sophomore year as it was a good Presbyterian co-educational college a few miles from Pasadena, in Eagle Rock, a part of Los Angeles. He was very much interested in philosophy and religion by now, and began to consider this to be his field of study. Occidental College offered two scholarships for Juniors at the University of Hawaii and Lingnan University in Canton, China. Walter applied for the exchange scholarship to Hawaii, and to his surprise was selected.

So he spent his junior year at the University of Hawaii studying Oriental religion, philosophy, and anthropology. The greatest event of that year, however, was meeting and studying with a great Quaker professor, Dr. Thomas R. Kelly. He had left Earlham College in Indiana, to be the only professor in the department of philosophy at Hawaii. Walter was his only major student, and he studied ethics, Western philosophy, and Chinese, Japanese, and

Indian religion and philosophy with Dr. Kelly. Most of all he was impressed with Kelly's Quaker views in religion, of man as a being who could go to God directly without intermediaries.

Walter Kring returned to Occidental for his Senior year, as he had agreed to do before he left. He continued his interest in public speaking and debating, and studied philosophy and religion. When he began to think about a graduate school, the pressures were on Walter Kring to enter the Presbyterian ministry. The Presbyterian seminaries at that time appeared to be too conservative for him. So at the suggestion of Dr. Elton Trueblood, another Quaker who was the chaplain at Stanford University, who came to Occidental for a religious emphasis week, he applied to the Harvard Divinity School, and was awarded a scholarship.

Later, as he looked back upon his college career, he was happy in the liberal Protestant religious tradition. He realized later that it was a course on ''The Trinity" taught by a wonderful Episcopalian woman dean that made him realize that he was really not a Trinitarian. When Occidental College awarded an honorary degree of Doctor of Humane Letters (L.H.D.) to Dr. Kring in 1965, he was most pleased. If he had been a Presbyterian minister he might have hoped for a Doctor of Divinity from Occidental, but as a Unitarian minister he had no hopes at all. The incredible happened on Founder's Day in 1965, and no recognition has ever meant more to Dr. Kring than this one by his own college to one who had strayed from the Presbyterian path.

Walter Kring went to Harvard Divinity School in the Fall of 1937, a rather shy, not too well educated (by Harvard standards) especially in language preparation. His class consisted of only eight men. He was the first person ever to go to Harvard Divinity School who was under the care of the rather conservative Boston Presbytery. He did some field work in a Congregational church in Belmont. Then, at the beginning of his second year at the Divinity School, Rev. Dr. Willard L. Sperry, the dean of the Divinity School, and the Preacher to the University, asked Walter Kring to assist him in the daily services at the college chapel, meeting the preachers, (often professors) going over the order of service with them, and listening to all of them preach. The next year, in addition to helping Dean Sperry, he became the student assistant at The First Church in Boston under one of the ablest Unitarian preachers, Dr. Charles Edwards Park, who taught a preaching class at the Divinity School.

Walter Kring graduated in the Divinity School Class of 1940. But being still undecided about his profession, he spent one more year at the school. He was trying to do a doctorate in comparative religions, but at that time Harvard really did not know how to give a doctorate in that field. (It is a leader in this field today.) He got bogged down in Sanscrit. The work with Langdon Warner in Far Eastern Art at the Fogg Museum was one of the major influences of his life, for from Langdon Warner Walter Kring learned to love Far Eastern art, particularly the ceramics. His study there led to his ceramic hobby which has been a joy all of his life. He had always loved to work with his hands, and he began what has been a life-long hobby of making pots and specializing in Oriental ceramic glazes.

At the end of four years at Harvard Walter Kring had a difficult decision to make. Should he stay at Harvard and try to finish the doctorate in work in which he didn't seem to be making much progress, or should he leave academia and try the ministry. He had enjoyed his work with Dr. Park at the First Church, but he had found Boston Unitarians liberal in religion and intensely conservative in everything else. When Dr. Park asked Walter if he were interested in being his full-time assistant minister, he felt that it was not for him.

Walter's mother was a great influence in encouraging him to return to the Presbyterian fold. So he candidated for a little Presbyterian church in Hoosick Falls, New York, and accepted a call. He had real difficulties in getting through an oral examination in front of Troy Presbytery, the members of which were right fully suspicious of his Harvard Divinity School and Unitarian connections. He was perfectly honest with them about his Christology, and for some reason, the Presbytery accepted him.

The ministry at Hoosick Falls was to be a short one because

that December the Japanese attacked Pearl Harbor and America was in World War II. It wasn't long before Walter Kring was practically the only young man left in the town. He served as cub master, scout master, and air scout master all at the same time. Although from his Quaker teachers he had strong feelings against war, he volunteered for the Naval Chaplaincy. He went to the Chaplain's School in Williamsburg, Virginia, after bidding good bye to his parish in Hoosick Falls. After about four months at the Chaplain's School Walter Kring was assigned to Del Monte, California, a delightful spot on the Monterey Peninsula which trained radar technicians. It was really a "plush lined foxhole." He preached to large congregations (1500 men). Chapel was compulsory, and he enjoyed his work with the bright young sailors.

Walter asked for aircraft carrier duty for his first assignment at sea, and received orders in January, 1945, to report to the U.S.S. "Shamrock Bay," which he was told was "somewhere in the Western Pacific." He found the carrier at Ulithi Atoll just after the "Shamrock Bay" had engaged in the Battle of Lingayan Gulf where 9 out of 18 of the small carriers had been damaged by kamikaze planes. During the battle of Iwo Jima the carrier flew air cover for the tanker fleet that daily refueled the fast carrier taskforce that was bombing Japan. Then after another rendezvous at Ulithi, the ship left a week before Easter to engage in a 90-day stint in the terrible battle of Okinawa. Here the pilots flew direct support for the marines on the ground. The crew saw many American ships that were damaged by the kamikazes, but fortunately the "Shamrock Bay" was never hit. It sailed back to the West Coast to San Francisco, and was in San Diego harbor when VJ Day arrived, with orders to join the fleet that was to invade Kyushu, the southernmost Island of Japan. That battle would have been a massacre that would have made Okinawa seem like child's play.

After the war ended the carrier became a troop transport, and transported troops from Okinawa, Japan, and Maui back to the United States. It was to be one of the most fortunate coincidences of Walter Kring's life that the "Shamrock Bay" was ordered to be decommissioned and be put in "mothballs" at the South Boston

Navy Yard. No one ever told the Irish of South Boston that Shamrock Bay was not in the old country as they assumed. The Navy had run out of names for ships, so someone took a map of Alaska and named many of the escort carriers for bays in Alaska. The Irish came down to the Navy Yard and claimed the "Shamrock Bay." Chaplain Kring became "Father O'Kring" to the Catholics of South Boston. There was no way to tell from the uniform insignia whether a chaplain was a Protestant or a Catholic.

While decomissioning in South Boston Walter Kring again made contacts with the First Church in Boston. Dr. Park was glad to see him, asked him to preach, and saw to it that a pulpit committee from the Second Church in Boston was there to hear him. This was the church of Henry Ware Jr. and Ralph Waldo Emerson. Chaplain Kring was again uncertain as to what wanted to do. He had applied to the Yale Graduate School in the field of philosophy, had taken the Graduate Records Examination, and even had his household goods moved to New Haven for storage. Walter Kring did know that he did not want to return to the Presbyterian ministry. He had found sectarianism too narrow. He preached several times at the Second Church, and they wanted to extend a call to him. But the last time he preached there he discovered to his surprise that there was a pulpit committee from the First Unitarian Church in Worcester, Massachusetts. They wanted him to visit Worcester.

Walter went out to Worcester and met the minister, Dr. Maxwell Savage, who had just completed 27 years as the minister of the church, and had built the church into one of the largest in the Unitarian denomination. He was the son of Minot Savage, a famous Unitarian minister, and a brother-in-law of Minot Simons, for many years the minister of All Souls, New York. The Worcester church was too large and important for a person with his meager experience. Walter Kring never would have sought that church. But to his surprise, they sought him - a thirty-year-old Presbyterian to be their minister. He began his ministry in Worcester in September, 1946.

It was a tremendous job for one so young. Kring should have

had more parish experience. But he and the people got along well, and the only unhappy time that he had with the Worcester people was when he told them after nine years of ministry that he had been called to All Souls Church in New York City, and he expected to accept the call.(7)

The New Ministry Begins

Walter Donald Kring became the eighth minister of the Unitarian Church of All Souls on Sunday evening, November 20, 1955. Chester Lane, the president of the board of trustees, conducted the Installation Ceremony. The Rev. Dr. Frederick May Eliot, president of the American Unitarian Association, gave the Charge to the Minister. Dr. Neale gave the Charge to the Congregation. There were many many guests of honor; practically all of the Unitarian ministers in greater New York attended.(8)

A Potter Shapes All Souls

No account of Walter Kring's ministry would be complete without some mention of his distinguished work as a potter. Interest in this hobby began at Harvard graduate school when he took a course in "Chinese and Japanese Art" from Langdon Warner, a distinguished orientalist. He became extremely interested in the Sung period of Chinese history, the celadon glazes (blues and greens) and the ox-blood glazes (bright red) that adorn so many ceramic pieces in museums.

When he went to his first parish in Hoosick Falls, he built a primitive kiln in the back yard. After settling in Worcester after the war, Mr. Kring built a high temperature kiln and made thousands of experiments to recreate these Oriental glazes. A trip to Japan in 1953 had only whetted his pleasure from these ceramics. One of his ox-blood bowls won a first prize in the National Ceramic Show in 1954. He displayed many of his pots in American

Adlai Stevenson, Presidential candidate, arrives at All Souls during the 1956 Presidential Campaign. Left to right: Mr. Stevenson's son, Eleanor Clark French, Mr. Stevenson, and Dr. Kring.

museums while minister at the Worcester church.

When he was called to New York, the chairman of the search committee told Mr. Kring that he was concerned about his hobby if he lived in New York City. Walter Kring thought that the committee believed his hobby would interfere with his more important church work. Quite the opposite, the committee was concerned that he continue his work, but felt that it might be difficult in the city. Dr. Kring has continued with his hobby to this day throwing many pots on the wheel, and entering exhibitions and shows.

Not only was he interested in crafting Oriental glazes but Mr. Kring was one of the founders of the modern Worcester Craft Center, and served as its first vice-president. In New York City he was twice the president of the Artist Craftsmen of New York, serving for a total of five years. He showed pots at the Metropolitan Museum of Art and the Smithsonian Institute in New York, was an exhibitor at the American Pavilion at the Brussels World's Fair, and has exhibited in several dozen other American museums. He was able, largely due to a long summer vacation, to continue his hobby all through his ministry at All Souls. So how did this potter shape All Souls?

Walter Kring's ministry was to last twenty-three years, the second longest ministry in the history of All Souls. The best way to look at the events of this nearly quarter of a century is to examine them under various areas of church concern. This gives a clearer picture of what happened during those years from 1955 until 1978 far better than a chronological account of the events.

Devotional Life of the Church

Mr. Kring believed that the most important aspect of the program of a church was public worship. An important step in the liturgical life of the church was taken when a special hymnbook committee completed its work in 1957. The committee prepared five regular opening services, and special services for Christmas, Easter, and Thanksgiving. There were also services for the Right

Hand of Fellowship (taking new members into the church) and a Christening ceremony. Also some prayers were added to the hymnbook. This special supplement was bound into the regular Unitarian hymnbook of the time, *The Hymns of the Spirit,* thus assuring some continuity in the worship services.

Members of the church volunteered to give one or more hymnbooks to the church at a cost of $4 a copy. The congregation responded enthusiastically. Present and former members of the board of trustees gave over 100 of the new hymnbooks in memory of Mark Walton Maclay. The hymnbooks were first used on Sunday, September 29, 1957. The hymnbook is still used at morning services.

During Kring's ministry there were attempts to get away from the usual kind of service of worship. Over the years a number of special worship services were held using music as the theme of the worship experience. The year 1956 marked the two hundredth anniversary of the birth of Wolfgang Amadeus Mozart. In honor of the anniversary on December 2, Mr. Kring preached on the subject of "Creative Genius," and William Brewster, the organist and choir director, played Mozart compositions, and the choir sang "Ave Verum" and a selection from Mozart's "Mass in C. Minor," the "Et Incarnatus Est."

On Sunday, February 21, 1971, Dr. Kring used music from the popular folk opera "Jesus Christ Superstar," and wove a sermon around the music. This was highly successful, and according to many persons who did not even like the music, it was very moving. So many persons requested a repeat performance that Dr. Kring gave the sermon again on April 9, which was Good Friday evening.

Gustav Mahler was the composer featured on Sunday morning, April 25, 1971. Dr. Kring presented another special sermon entitled; "Religious Moods of Gustav Mahler." He had taped excerpts from all of the ten Mahler symphonies and "Das Lied von der Erde." The music was interrupted with interpretation, and lasted a long 45 minutes. Again, the response was excellent. But, as Dr. Kring pointed out to the worship commission which asked for more similar sermons, it takes a long time to put together such a sermon. On Sunday, December 26, 1971, at the morning service, Dr. Kring played a cut version of Leonard Bernstein's "Mass" which had just been presented at the opening of the Kennedy Center in Washington, D. C. In the afternoon, Schuyler Chapin, who at the time was Mr,. Bernstein's manager, and who had made the early copy of the tape available, joined with Dr. Kring to present the whole of the "Mass" to the congregation. It lasted an hour and a half. Dr. Kring wrote about the "Mass" in the church calendar:

My impression of the "Mass" is that it is a major work of our era. It combines hauntingly beautiful folk music with orchestral interludes that are Mahlerian in impact, marching bands with rock and blues. It is thoroughly contemporary, and yet it brings to the traditional Catholic Mass and its Latin words a modern relevance that is most moving. It is important that you not just listen to the "Mass" but experience it."(9)

On Sunday morning, February 29, 1976, Dr. Kring presented another musical sermon. This time it was a little more esoteric than the Mahler program, for it was the playing of the works of Alexander Scriabin, whose music is little known. Scriabin wrote five symphonies, and outlined, but never finished, a sixth. The sermon described the varying moods of the music, and its spiritual significance.

On April 16, 1976, Good Friday, Dr. Kring conducted an all afternoon program in the church for persons to come into the sanctuary to listen, and to meditate. The program lasted from noon until the benediction was pronounced at 4:40 P.M. Dr. Kring in troduced and played the five symphonies of Alexander Scriabin, and the reconstructed sixth symphony of Scriabin. Scriabin left only notes and scribbles of his musical ideas, and a modern Russian composer, Alexander Nemtin, filled in the missing places and made a symphony out of it. Scriabin called it "The Mysterium," and he is said to have believed that when it was played the world would come to an end, a apocalyptic symphony. It was a highly unorthodox, Good Friday service, but several hundred people came in during the afternoon. and many stayed throughout the almost five hours.

Dance was also an element introduced into the worship services. For the Christmas season in 1966, Charles Weidman, an out standing master of modern dance and a student of Martha Graham, brought his dance troupe into the church sanctuary on Tuesday evening, December 27, and led the group in a two-hour dance program to the music of "The Christmas Oratorio" by Johann Sebastian Bach.

On Sunday morning, January 26, 1976, a most unusual service took place, again encouraged by the worship commission. Vija Vetra, who had presented a dance program in Fellowship Hall previously, danced several numbers of Indian dance while Dr. Kring read some of Rabindranath Tagore's poetry, accompanied by cello and organ. It was a most satisfying combination of worship and aesthetics, and was much appreciated by the congregation.

Ecumenical Outreach

Dr. Kring and the parishioners also believed that there should be a constant attempt to reach out to other religious groups in the community. Typical of many such efforts were events such as these.

The Universalist Church of the Divine Paternity and All Souls combined for a Union Thanksgiving Service on Thanksgiving Day, November 22, 1956, at All Souls Church. The All Souls Choir sang several anthems, and the Rev. Albert Ciarcia, the minister of the Universalist church, preached the sermon. These Thanksgiving Ecumenical services continued for some years, and late in Dr. Kring's ministry other churches and synagogues were included in such Thanksgiving services.

In September 1968, Dr. Donald Harrington of the Community

Church, and Dr. Kring exchanged pulpits for the first time in either of their pastorates, and probably for the first time since before John Haynes Holmes became the minister of the Community Church in 1907. They decided to both preach on the subject; "How My Ideas of God Have Changed in the Past 25 Years." On Sunday, September 22, Dr. Kring preached his sermon to the All Souls congregation. Donald Harrington did likewise to his congregation. The next week they exchanged pulpits, and preached the same sermon to each other's congregations.

At the meeting of the All Souls Guild after church on Sunday November 12, 1967, Dr. Kring and Father John Campbell, a Dominican priest, conducted a completely unrehearsed dialogue on the common areas of belief and disbelief between the Unitarian and Roman Catholic faiths. The Roman Catholic priests in the East Mid-Town area, in the new spirit of ecumenism, had joined with members of the East Mid-Town Ministers Association, of which Dr. Kring had been the president. It was a new show of good spirit much appreciated by all.

In September 1968, the church offered its facilities to th National Federation of Temple Brotherhoods for the celebration of the Jewish High Holy Days. The services were open to all Jewish students at local colleges and universities, hospitals, etc. who did not have a home temple which they could attend to celebrate the High Holy Days. The church was filled to capacity on two occasions that year. These services continued each year at the Jewish High Holy Days.

On Sunday, May 23, 1971, Dr. Kring moved into the chancel a glass altarpiece that he had constructed some years earlier, and which then hung in the All Souls School. The altarpiece was designed and constructed with a definite philosophy of comparative religions in mind. The ten symbols of the major world religions were touching each other, indicating the one great family of all mankind. the symbols in the altarpiece were the Christian cross, the Hebrew star of David, the Buddhist lotus, the Chinese symbol of the Tao, the altar and fire of Zoroaster, the star and crescent of the Moslem religion, the Shinto torii, the Yin and the Yang of Chinese religion, and the eight hexagrams of Chinese religion, and the Chinese characters of Kung Fu Tze, or Confucius. The sermon was on the subject "How Religion Can Bind the World Together."

That same year, Mrs. Edward Avildsen wrote a new Christmas pageant, and her brother-in-law, John Avildsen, who later became a renowned Hollywood movie director, directed it. One of the innovations this year was that the pageant was written in a very informal style. While the minister was explaining the miracle of the rebirth of the seed in the Spring, one of the members of the cast sitting in the congregation, interrupted Dr. Kring to ask a question. So real was the acting and so effective was the script that many people thought that the "interruption" was for real. One of the trustees got up from his pew and approached the questioner and asked him to desist, and another trustee headed down the aisle for the same purpose.

The purpose of the interruption was to enable one of the young people in the cast to explain why the birth of Jesus is celebrated, and it was done most effectively. Following the pageant, carols were sung, and a Christmas tree was decorated in Fellowship Hall in memory of Dr. Charles Theodore Christian Pollen, acting minister of All Souls from 1836-1838, who had re-introduced the decorated Christmas tree in America at his home in Cambridge, Massachusetts.

The Congregation Discusses Religious Symbolism

All during Walter Kring's ministry at All Souls the symbolism of the cross above the pulpit was a source of controversy. There were very strong feelings pro and con as to whether this was an appropriate symbol for a Unitarian church. When the church had first been built in 1932 at Eightieth Street and Lexington Avenue, there had been no symbolism. But in 1940, Dr. Simons, concerned about the war that was then raging in Europe, asked the board of trustees if he could hang the cross from the old "Holy Zebra" church in the chancel for the Easter service.

The cross remained. The congregation was divided down the middle about the symbolism of the cross. All Souls had between 20 and 25 percent of its members who came from Jewish background. These former Jewish members were just as divided as the rest of the congregation on the matter of the symbolism of the cross. It was the beginning of a discussion that was to go on for almost a decade. But in order to begin the thinking process of the congregation, Dr. Kring preached on the subject "Shall We Remove the Cross from Our Church," on November 30, 1969.

A model of the church chancel was made, and many suggestions were received from members of the congregation as to the proper symbolism. By 1977, the discussion about the church symbolism had reached a point where some decision had to be made. It was agreed that the cross would be removed from the chancel pending a decision by the congregation. After hearing the suggestions of the congregation, the worship commission now presented a series of suggestions on the model of the chancel in Fellowship Hall. There was to be a non-binding straw vote on which of the suggestions the congregation liked the best. On December 4, Dr. Kring preached a sermon on "Symbolism," and the attendants were asked to come with their prejudices about symbolism, but also with an open mind. It had been determined that this was not going to be a controversy that would develop into an issue that would divide the congregation. So votes were not taken until there was some degree of unanimity.(10) The issue was not resolved until Dr. Kring's successor was already in the pulpit.

Support for the Unitarian Universalist Service Committee

One of the happy events during Dr. Kring's ministry was the remarkable support given by All Souls people to the work of the Unitarian Service Committee, and its successor the Unitarian Universalist Service Committee. Leadership of the campaign was in the capable hands of Peter I. B. Lavan. In 1956, for instance, All Souls gave the largest contribution to the

Unitarian Service Committee of any church in the denomination, five times the amount contributed by the second ranking church. In 1957, All Souls contributed $20,000 to the Service Committee's work, and over the next years these large amounts continued to pour in. At one time in the sixties, the John Lindsley Fund, whose executive trustee was Dr. Kring, gave $25,000 to the Service Committee in a single contribution.

The Death of Dr. Frederick May Eliot

On Sunday morning, February 16, 1958, Dr. Frederick May Eliot, the president of the American Unitarian Association, preached at All Souls Church while Mr. Kring was preaching at Cornell University. Dr. Eliot had an appointment the following morning at 9 o'clock with Mr. Kring to discuss some problems of the Beacon Press of which Mr. Kring was the president of the board. Dr. Eliot came out of the subway at the Seventy-Seventh Street station and walked the three short blocks to the entrance of the Memorial Garden. But when he reached the gate he was stricken with a fatal heart attack and fell to the ground just inside the garden gate. Miss Mrytle Crooks, the minister's secretary, was on the lookout for Dr. Eliot, and she saw him fall. A physician who lived nearby was summoned, but there was nothing that could be done. Dr. Eliot had suffered a massive heart attack, and died instantly.

Mr. Kring's train from Ithaca was delayed by a heavy snow storm, and when he arrived at the church shortly before noon, Dr. Eliot's body was still there, awaiting transportation back to Boston. Dr. Eliot was a kind of symbol of Unitarianism. Sometimes he was spoken of as "Mr. Unitarian." After a very successful pastorate at Saint Paul, Minnesota, Dr. Eliot had responded to the call to be the president of the Association. He had served in this capacity for twenty-one years. Mr. Kring had served with Dr. Eliot as secretary of the American Association for some five years when Dr. Eliot died. It was a close relationship, and although they didn't always agree on some matters, they respected each other deeply.

All Souls Buys A "Dead Sea Scroll"

In 1958, All Souls assisted in the purchase of one of the frag ments of the Dead Sea Scrolls through the generosity of Mr. Thayer Lindsley. As Mr. Kring described it:

> *To show the kind of a world in which we live - it is interest-ing that a Hebrew manuscript should have been purchased by a Frenchman and an American (A Catholic priest, and a Presbyterian) from Moslems, to be deposited in a museum in an Arab country (Jordan), with funds made available through a Unitarian Church, during a severe political cri-sis. Such are the ways of God and men. We are proud to have had a hand in this significant discovery and purchase.*

This small scroll turned out to be the oldest complete copy in Hebrew of the Ten Commandments, and the scholars called it in honor of the church, "The All Souls Deuteronomy." It was later dated at about the time of Jesus, 1 A.D. It was somewhat unusual as a scroll for it contained a merger of the two versions of the Ten Commandments found in Exodus and Deuteronomy, particularly about the reasons for the observance of the Sabbath.(11)

Hospitality for Two Jewish Synagogues

During these years All Souls hosted two Jewish syna-gogues. In 1958, Congregation Shaaray Tefila faced a problem. This congregation, located on West 82nd Street on the West side of Manhattan, celebrated its centenary in 1945. But the congreation of this Reformed synagogue had largely moved to the East side of Manhattan. They sold the old building and bought a theatre at the corner of 79th Street and Second Av-enue. The problem was where they would meet while the the-atre was being renovated. The board of trustees of All Souls on behalf of the congregation invited the congregation of Shaaray

Tefila to use the facilities of All Souls during this period on Friday evenings, Saturday mornings, and during the Jewish High Holy Days. It was a good relationship in more ways than just being good neighbors. They used the facilities of All Souls for almost a full year, and then they moved into their new synagogue which in no way now resembled a movie theatre.(12)

They proved to be not only considerate but generous guests. Notwithstanding that they came without any financial commitment, Dr. Kring announced the receipt from them of a check for $2,500 accompanied by a handsome illuminated scroll which now hangs in the foyer of the church.

At the annual meeting Samuel M. Lane, the president of the trustees, showed the congregation the scroll and read the inscription which expressed the deep gratitude for the church's generous hospitality. "You helped to assure the survival of our Congregation in a critical period... Your actions are a noble example of true Brotherhood."(13)

Several years later, in 1962, Miss Florence McKinlay, the first woman president of the board of trustees, announced that a second Reformed temple, Temple Israel, would begin to use the church's facilities shortly as Temple Shaaray Tefila had in the past. They had bought a plot of land on East 75th Street near the church, and planned to build a temple shortly.

On Friday, February 15, 1963, the Men's Club of Temple Israel made its annual "Man-of-the-Year Brotherhood Award" to Dr. Kring. Colonel Arthur Leavitt, comptroller of the State of New York, gave the citation. Undoubtedly, the church itself should have received the award, for it was a token of appreciation from Temple Israel for All Souls offering them a temporary home while constructing their new temple.

The temple encountered difficulties in getting their new temple constructed. When the excavation was made for the foundation, a hidden river was discovered. Then there was a strike for six months by one of the unions. The new leader of the temple, Rabbi Martin J. Zion, preached at the All Souls service on March 13, 1966, and thanked the congregation for their patience in hosting the temple.

The congregation of All Souls was invited to visit the newly opened temple on Friday evening, May 20. Dr. Kring was the preacher of the evening. The temple presented the church with an illuminated plaque which now hangs in the foyer of the church in appreciation of the hosting of their services at All Souls. In part it read: "May we continue to dwell together in unity to make our world a sanctuary of brotherhood and peace."(14)

The "Suspense of Faith"

On June 7, 1959, Mr. Kring observed the hundredth anniversary of a great address called "The Suspense of Faith," delivered at the Harvard Divinity School by Henry Whitney Bellows. This sermon has been considered one of the landmarks of preaching in the nineteenth century. In it Dr. Bellows described the loss of faith in religious institutions, and was somewhat misunderstood when he called for a new "catholic" church, by which he meant a liberal universal church that would shut no one out.(15)

John Kennedy Memorial Service

On Sunday, November 24, 1963, the order of service was changed in order that there might be a memorial service for President John F. Kennedy who had been assassinated the previous Thursday. Dr. Kring preached on "The President; An Appreciation." The church was filled to overflowing not just with church members but with many people not associated with All Souls but wanted to make an expression of respect for the martyred President. The next day at noon, All Souls Church, and Temple Israel held another Memorial Service for President Kennedy. It was an ecumenical service with Rabbi William F. Rosenblum, soon to be Rabbi Emeritus of Temple Israel in January, Rabbi Martin J. Zion, the new Rabbi of Temple Israel, Cantor Jonas I. Javna, and Dr. Kring participating. There were prayers, three minutes of silence,

The 150th Anniversary Celebration on November 16, 1969.
Photo: George E. Joseph.

Participants in the 150th Anniversary Celebration. From left to right: Edward N. Costikyan, Moderator; Dr. Kring, Reverend Charles Taylor, Rabbi Martin J. Zion, Dean Kister Stendahl, and Dr. Donald Harrington of the Community Church. Photo: George E. Joseph.

the quartet of Temple Israel sang "Ave Verum" of Mozart, and the cantor sang several numbers.

Twenty Five Years in the Ministry

On September 11, 1966, Dr. Kring celebrated twenty-five years in the ministry. He preached on the subject; "A Retrospect - Twenty-Five Years in the Ministry." On the back page of the church calendar for that week Dr. Kring wrote something about his impressions of a visit to the Holy Land that summer:

What struck me as the most formidable barrier was not this overlay of tradition but the fact that for many persons today Jesus, the prophet of Nazareth, is not only not known but irrelevant."(16)

The 150th Anniversary

At the 1968 annual meeting, Dr. Kring announced preliminary plans for the celebration of the 150th anniversary of the founding of the church in November, 1819, and he also announced a special gift from the John Lindsley Fund for the publication of the history of the church which he was then writing.

The one hundred and fiftieth anniversary was now at hand. On Sunday, November 9, 1969, Dr. Kring preached an historical sermon on Dr. Charles Theodore Christian Follen, a German refugee Transcendentalist who had been the acting minister of All Souls Church from 1836-1838. On Thursday November 13, Ralph Miller, director of the Museum of the City of New York, and a member of All Souls, gave an illustrated lecture on "The Beginning of Greatness, New York City in 1819, Its Social, Political, and Economic Life." On Friday, November 14, there was a dinner dance at the Hotel Pierre, attended by about 200 per sons. The John Lindsley Fund had contributed some much needed funds for the celebration of the anniversary, so that an event like this was possible.

At the regular Sunday morning service on Sunday November 16, Dr. Kring preached a sermon on the life of All Souls greatest minister, Dr. Henry Whitney Bellows. The All Souls Guild joined in the festivities in having a special program celebrating the anniversary. On that same afternoon at 5, there was a special anniversary service. The preacher for the service was Dr. Krister Stendahl, the dean of the Harvard Divinity School, and a leading New Testament scholar. Dr. Stendahllater became the Bishop of the Swedish Church in Stockholm, Sweden, and is now the Chaplain at Harvard Divinity School.

Also featured at the anniversary service was a commissioned work for chorus and classical guitar by Daniel Pinkham, noted American composer, and organist and choir director at King's Chapel in Boston. A commemorative plate with a picture of the church and the names and dates of the ministers had been prepared for the anniversary, and was on sale.

Arthur Holden, a noted architect and member of All Souls, had written a sonnet celebrating William Ellery Channing's visit to New York in 1819, and the founding of All Souls Church, which was printed in the anniversary program. Dr. Kring gave the opening prayer, Edward Costikyan, the president of the board of trustees, welcomed the congregation and the visitors and distinguished guests to the service. Rabbi Martin Zion, of Temple Israel, read the Old Testament lesson, Reverend Charles Taylor, pastor of nearby St. Ignatius Loyola Roman Catholic Church, read the New Testament lesson. Dr. Stendahl's address "The Church Is Always In the Making," came next on the program. Dr. Donald Harrington gave the anniversary prayer, the choir and a guitarist performed the Daniel Pinkham composition, led by the composer, and after a recessional, Dr. Kring gave the benediction.

Dr. Kring had also written "A Brief Sketch of the Founding of All Souls," which was printed in the program. Dr. Kring earlier in the Fall had explained to the members of the church, that although he had been delegated by the trustees to write the one hundred-

and-fiftieth-anniversary book of the church's history, many things had transpired to delay the publication of the book. Six months before the anniversary he had thought that the book was completed, and he had read it aloud to Jeanne Walton, who was the researcher. It was a "once over lightly" history of the church.

But one day Raphael Torres, the sexton, told Dr. Kring that he had forgotten to tell him that there was a safe in a closet off Fellowship Hall which had a lot of documents in it. This safe when opened was a "gold mine" of material about the history of the church, and this new material simply made the present working copy of the history totally inadequate. For example, there was the list of members of the church prepared in 1885 by Rev. Theodore Chickering Williams, which it was later discovered contained the name of Herman Melville.

Lay Assistance at the Morning Service

As a part of the one hundred and fiftieth anniversary celebration a committee had been appointed to look ahead and plan for the next twenty-five years. One of the outgrowths of their report was the establishment of a worship commission which aided Dr. Kring in the planning of the worship services. It was a very satisfactory advisory committee during the remainder of Dr. Kring's ministry. One of the things that appeared to be desired was that lay people take some part in the morning worship service. So for some months a layperson read one of the lessons. Eventually, many felt that the laypeople were simply doing what the minister should do in the service.

Finally, a new procedure was begun that is still used today. One of the members of the church opened the service by welcoming the congregation, and then speaking for three or four minutes about something that was on his or her mind, usually why they became a Unitarian, or were attracted to All Souls Church. The lay person then led the congregation in the reciting of the Bond of Union of the church. This proved to be a very

satisfactory addition to the service, and made it something more
than just the minister's service. It is obviously carried on today
because it was a good idea.

The General Assembly in New York in 1974

The General Assembly of the Unitarian Universalist Association met in New York City at the Americana Hotel, in June, 1974.
At the opening worship service on June 27, Dr. George Markey
led the All Souls Choir in singing several anthems. The Unitarian
Universalist Ministers Association conducted their annual meeting at All Souls, and at the luncheon meeting when Dr. Kring told
the group that it was now fairly certain that it had been discovered
that Herman Melville was a genuine member of All Souls, he was
warmly applauded.(17) There were two hundred ministers present, and they were served a Szechuan Chinese luncheon from a
nearby restaurant. Mary-Ella Zipple was in charge of hospitality
for the convention, and Sandra Caron, as president of the Metropolitan District, was in charge of the overall organization. Many
of the members of All Souls served on the various committees,
and worked at the conference.

The Bicentennial Celebration

On Sunday April 25, 1976 to honor the country's bicenten-
nial, a special service entitled "Unitarian Poets" was presented,
again at the urging of the worship commission. Arthur Holden,
All Souls "Poet Laureate," read his poem about Channing's vis-
it to New York City titled "A New Spirit" to open the service.
Selections from Henry Wadsworth Longfellow, Ralph Waldo
Emerson, Eliza Cabot Follen, Herman Melville, William Cullen
Bryant, Amy Lowell, E. E. Cummings, and an original poem by
Mary-Ella Zippel, were read by members of the congregation.
Of these poets, Eliza Cabot Follen, Herman Melville, William

Cullen Bryant, and Mary-Ella Zippel, had some connection with All Souls Church. The readings were done by Mary-Ella Zippel, Peter Avildsen, Jonathan Sinclair Carey, and Dr. Kring.

Three Ordinations

During Dr. Kring's ministry there were three services of ordination at All Souls Church. At a special meeting of the congregation held on Wednesday evening, May 8, 1957, Webster Lardner Kitchell was called to be the associate minister of All Souls Church. He was to be graduated from Harvard Divinity School in June, and he would begin his work at the church on the first of August. On Sunday evening, October 13, Mr. Kitchell was ordained and installed as the associate minister of All Souls. Rev. Carl R. Scovel gave the invocation and Lord's Prayer, Rev. Charles Reinhardt of Staten Island read the evening lesson, Dr. James Luther Adams, professor at the Harvard Divinity School, delivered the sermon. Raymond S. Fanning, president of the board of trustees, led the congregation in the service of ordination and installation. Mr. Kring gave the ordination prayer. The Right Hand of Fellowship was given by Rev. Donald W McKinney, minister of the Church of the Savior in Brooklyn. The charge to the minister was given by Rev. Heinz Rettig, minister of the First Parish Church in Taunton, Massachusetts. Mr. Kring gave the charge to the congregation. Greetings were brought by Rev. Raymond B. Johnson, representing the A.U.A., and Dr. Dale DeWitt, the regional director of the A.U.A. Mr. Kitchell gave the benediction.

On Sunday, June 1, 1969, the All Souls congregation had the unusual privilege to ordain one of their own members. Dr. Charles Slap had finished his work at Meadville, and had been called to be the minister of the Unitarian Fellowship of Greater Lafayette, Indiana. He chose to be ordained in his home church. Dr. Kring preached the sermon on "Why the Ministry?" and Edward Costikyan, as the president of the board of trustees, led the congregation in the service of ordination; "By the authority and consent of the members of The Church of All Souls, we do hereby ordain you, Charles Slap, to the Ministry of Religion." The Rev. Dr. Charles Solomon Slap gave the benediction. Dr. Slap is now the minister of the First Unitarian Society of Schenectady, New York.

Having voted to ordain him, on June 5, 1977, the congregation proceeded to the ordination of Jonathan Sinclair Carey. Dr. Bert Zippel opened the service. The Old Testament lesson was read by Rev. Dr. James Hasting Nichols, academic dean, Princeton Theological Seminary. The New Testament lesson was read by Rev. Dr. Thomas P. O'Malley, S.J., dean of the College, Boston College. The sermon was delivered by Rev. Dr. James L. McCord, president of Princeton Theological Seminary. Dr. McCord then read a testimonial from Princeton Theological Seminary, and Dr. Kring read a testimonial from the Unitarian Church of All Souls on the suitability of Mr. Carey to be ordained. Marianne Roffman, president of the board of trustees and of the congregation, then questioned Jonathan Carey concerning his intentions in being ordained. She then asked the congregation "to vocally affirm his ordination," which the congregation did.

Rev. Carl Scovel, minister of King's Chapel, conducted a ceremony of consecration and the laying on of hands, a service in which all of the ministers participated. This was an unusual part of a Unitarian ordination ceremony, but it had been requested by Mr. Carey. Mrs. Roffman then read a prayer of consecration and right hand of fellowship which had come out of a sixth century Visigothic rite. Rev. Dr. Arlo D. Duba, director of admissions at Princeton Theological Seminary presented the symbols of the ministry. Dr. Kring gave a charge to the newly ordained minister, and Rev. Jonathan Sinclair Carey, as was the usual custom, pronounced the benediction. Jonathan Carey served the Eliot Church of South Natick (Federated) for two years, and then moved to Oxford, England, to seek a doctorate in medical ethics.

Associate Organizations

Although little mention has been made about the ongoing organizations within the church, at each annual meeting these organizations also reported. Some cognizance ought to be taken of these organizations. The Society for the Relief and Employment of Poor Women was founded in 1844, largely to provide sewing work for immigrant women. The New York Fruit and Flower Mission was founded in 1870 to distribute food to poor people at Christmas holidays. The Women's Alliance, founded in 1890, took responsibility for running the church fair, provided for about one-third of the coffee hours after church services, and provided hostesses for the Sunday services. It met regularly once a month. The Cheerful Letter Committee, founded in 1913, made pads for the Cancer Society and distributed toys at Christmas time. The American Red Cross Chapter was founded in 1915 during the First World War to roll bandages, and had continued since that time largely as a fundraising organization for the American Red Cross. The Unitarian Laymen's League, All Souls Chapter, met once a month for a dinner meeting with guest speakers. It had also sponsored an East Side Forum for debating political and social issues during and immediately after the Second World War.

The All Souls Guild was founded in 1922. It conducted Sunday luncheon meetings with programs. The average attendance had been 75 persons. The Unitarian Service Committee, All Souls Chapter, annually raised funds for the Unitarian Service Committee and its self-help projects all over the world. The Youth Activities Group, founded in 1954, was developing a constitution and had conducted discussion meetings and social evenings. The Church School Parents Association, founded in 1955, had 70 family memberships and ran a children's fair. The All Souls Business and Professional Women, founded in 1959, conducted supper meetings with speakers. In addition to these organizations, three other committees usually reported at the annual meetings; the Flower Committee was in charge of flowers for the Sunday services, the Guest Book Committee manned the guest book and tried to make visitors feel at home, and the Book Table Committee manned the book table at the coffee hours, and sold books published by the Beacon Press, and other books of special interest to Unitarians.

Denominational Issues

Two major denominational issues came before the congregation during Dr. Kring's tenure. One concerned the merger of the Unitarian and Universalist denominations; the other involved the issue of Black power.

Merger with the Universalists

On Tuesday evening, February 16, 1959, and continuing through April 7, the congregation held a series of meetings. These were the first of what during the next few years were to be many meetings on the question of the proposed merger of the Unitarian and the Universalist denominations. This was to be a merger on a national basis, not a local one. The sentiment of the congregation was divided, but many persons expressed anti-merger sentiments. The problem was that few members of the congregation knew much about the Universalist denomination even though the Universalist church across the Park often had joint Thanksgiving services with All Souls. Mr. Kring appeared on several platforms and wrote an article in the *Christian Register,* taking the anti-merger side of the issue.(18)

At the first meeting of the new board of trustees after the 1960 annual meeting, Chester Lane (no relation to Samuel M. Lane) was chosen to be the president. At the special meeting of the congregation feelings ran as high as they ever had since the beginning of Mr. Kring's ministry. By the time the final plan had been published, Mr. Kring and Samuel M. Lane had changed their opinion about the merger.

One of the things that had hampered the functioning of the American Unitarian Association was that the money was raised in a package called "The United Unitarian Appeal." Many organizations got their share of the funds, and many thought that the de nomination itself suffered from lack of funds. Under the new consolidation the denomination would raise its own funds rather than sharing with the Layman's League, the Women's National Alliance, and other groups. Mr. Kring with his seven years of experience on the board of directors of the association and on the executive committee, believed that the new organization would be stronger than the old one.

The main objection to the new consolidation in the minds of many was that they conceived the Universalist Church to be quite radical. Actually, by and large the Universalists were more conservative than the Unitarians in many matters. But several of their churches and outspoken ministers gave the denomination a bad name in the eyes of some of the members of All Souls. The vote at the special meeting was quite close; 147 for consolidation, 114 against the plan. So All Souls joined the ranks of those churches which approved the plan, but the internal struggle was deepened.

In his message in the calendar for March 27, 1960, Mr. Kring tried to assuage the fears of some members of the church who feared that if consolidation did go through (as it looked as if it would) that All Souls church would cease to be the Unitarian Church of All Souls. Mr. Kring pointed out that in our doctrine of the church each congregation is completely independent. Nor was the new consolidation going to be called "The Liberal Church of America," as some feared. The new organization would be called The Unitarian Universalist Association, and he pointed out that nothing locally would be changed at All Souls. Since the required number of Unitarian and Universalist churches had not yet voted in favor of consolidation this was still a period of uncertainty and doubt.

On Tuesday evening, March 22, 1960, a special meeting of the congregation was held to determine whether the vote of the delegates to the next meeting of the American Unitarian Association would be instructed how to vote on this matter, and whether the vote should be in the proportion that the congregation had voted, or if the entire delegation should be instructed to vote for consolidation. At this meeting by a vote of 154 to 95, the congregation decided that the All Souls delegates to the May Meetings of the Association were instructed to vote 100% for consolidation. They were left uninstructed as usual in matters other than this.

The Issue of Black Power

The late 1960's were a period in American history when the race problems had spiraled with burning of blocks in the inner cities. After the assassination of the Rev. Martin Luther King, Jr., there had been a resurgence among many blacks of what was termed "Black Power." This movement threatened to burst into open flame in the continental Unitarian Universalist denomination where a group of blacks, backed by many white ministers and lay people, were demanding that blacks be given a large sum of money to begin Black Power projects. On Sunday, April 28, 1966, Dr. Kring preached on the subject "Black, White, or Human," in which he outlined the way of integration as the Unitarian ideal in race relations as opposed to "Black Power."

Dr. Kring and the delegation from All Souls attended the General Assembly of the Unitarian Universalist Association in Cleveland, Ohio, from May 23 - 30,1966. There a group of blacks and whites had demanded that a million dollars be appropriated for "Black Power" projects. The All Souls delegation still believed that "Black Power" was not the way that Unitarian Universalists ought to face up to the racial situation. But the meeting in Cleveland was presented with a "take it or leave it," situation, and the majority of the delegates voted to go along with the Black Power Group. Dr. Kring announced that on Sunday June 9 he would preach a sermon on the subject. But that week on June 6, Robert Kennedy was assassinated in San Francisco, and the program was changed to a service of remembrance, and Dr. Kring preached on "Violence As a Way of Life." The country had been thoroughly shaken by the assassinations of John Kennedy, Rev. Martin Luther King, Jr., and now Robert Kennedy.

But on Sunday, June 16, the sermon subject was announced in the calendar with a black band of mourning, and these words, "Dr. Kring believes that our denomination reached the end of an era at Cleveland, and that new thrusts are needed to bring denominational sanity." The subject announced was "Is There a Phoenix Among Unitarian Universalist Ashes?" The sermon expressed the great concern of those who had attended the convention that the denomination had taken a step that was completely Un-Unitarian. The sermon was later printed and distributed to all of the churches in the denomination; one of the few sermons given that month which took this side of the subject, and, as some said, dared to face the realities of the situation.

Taking as his text Matthew 7:15: "Beware of false prophets, who come to you in sheep's clothing, but inwardly are ravenous wolves. You will know them by their fruits," Dr. Kring recounted what had happened at Cleveland, and said that he had never seen such differences between people at the continental convention. The convention recognized by a vote of 836 to 327 a Black Affairs Council, and the delegates voted a sum of $250,000 a year for four years to fund "Black Power" projects, and there was to be no accounting of how the money had been spent. Dr. Kring felt that the convention had taken sides in the black community, and that the Unitarian principle of integration (so that eventually the color of one's skin would not matter) was the proper position for Unitarians.

He quoted Dr. Harrington of the Community Church of New York, who said; 'The result was, in my view, a sickening embracing of counter-revolution in the name of revolution, of segregation in the name of integration, of vice in the name of virtue." Incidentally, the Community Church was probably the best racially integrated church in the denomination, and a full delegation of its black members were there speaking against the "Black Power" concept. For the first time that anyone could remember since the First World War, All Souls and The Community Church were on the same side of an important issue.

The church calendar for October 13, 1968, contained a statement by the board of trustees in regard to the newly formed Black Affairs Council. The board wisely stated that it would not commit the church to any specific position. But they strongly urged the denominational affairs committee and the congregation in general to study the activities of the Council to see what position, if any, the church should take. It was signed by all nine of the trustees.

With the 1969 General Assembly of the Unitarian Universalist Association only a few months away, the discussion about the Black Power Group was heating up. On April 27, Dr. Kring preached on the subject; "Can Rational Man Negotiate Irrational Demands?" It was announced by the board of trustees that instead of having one congregational meeting to discuss the denomination, that it had been thought best that there be three meetings.

On April 29, the meeting discussed what the denominations did and how it spent its money. This was essentially an instructional meeting. The May 13 meeting discussed whether gifts to the Unitarian Universalist Association denomination should be put in the church budget rather than follow the present method of individual giving. It was decided to follow the present arrangement. The third meeting on May 27 was called to discuss whether the church's delegates to the Boston meeting should be instructed as to how to vote, and if so, how they should be instructed. The denomination was in bad financial shape. Not only was there the annual gift to the Black Power Group, but most of the general endowment funds of the denomination had been spent in the last few years. The congregation did not instruct its delegates, but they were aware quite vividly as to how the congregation felt about the situation within the denomination.

In the midst of all of the discussion about race relations, the congregation of All Souls decided to extend a hand of friendship to a black church. It was discovered that there was an All Souls Episcopal Church in Harlem. It was composed largely of people from the island of Jamaica. On May 18, Father Clifford S. Lauder, the pastor, came to All Souls and preached the sermon. The next week on May 25, Dr. Kring went to All Souls Episcopal Church in Harlem on St. Nicholas Avenue, and preached the sermon. While Dr. Kring was absent, Charles Slap, who was to be ordained by the congregation the next Sunday, preached at All Souls. It was an interesting exchange. Father Lauder's sermon topic was "Jesus

Is Lord," and Dr. Kring said that during the very high Episcopal service in Harlem the censor took special care to see that he was well fumigated. It was the beginning of a productive relationship between the two churches.

With so much at stake in the Unitarian Universalist Association, the church chose some of its strongest denomination al people to go to the 1969 meetings in Boston; Sandra Caron, W. Stephens Dietz, Francisca P. Ehrenclou, Mrs. Arne H. Groningsater, Walter H. Hindle, Mrs. Murray S. Leigh, Mrs. Jerome Mayer, Miss Florence McKinlay, Dr. Grace Spofford, and Mrs. M. Lauck Walton, in addition to Dr. Kring.

In the church calendar for September 21, Dr. Kring wrote about some of his impressions of the July meeting. He felt that the only things religious about the meetings were the well-attended worship services led by ministers and laymen. There was placed before the meeting a demand for ten million dollars in Black reparations, but that motion fell flat. Realizing that the demand would be soundly defeated, the motion was withdrawn. Dr. Kring wrote:

The thing that most disturbed the delegates was that some of the white ministers attempted to cut off debate at the assembly by seizing the microphones and hiding them in their coats, a most un-Unitarian procedure, at best.

Dr. Kring believed, along with the most of the All Soul's delegates, that our non-creedal denomination had now become creedal in regard to some social actions and political opinions. The assembly by a rather narrow vote refused to admit that there is more than one way for blacks and whites to work together in a church. A new organization was to be founded called BAWA (Black and White Action) as a result of these meetings, as a counter-measure.

Dr. Kring concluded his remarks with these words:

My feeling is that in another year we may be back in the tradition of Unitarian open-mindedness in matters social and economic as well as religious, but Unitarian-Universalists have a long way to go before we will attract new people to our midst on the basis of religious concepts.(19)

On February 6, 1970, Father Clifford Lauder brought 125 of the members of the All Soul's Episcopal Church in Harlem down to All Soul's Unitarian Church, and together with 125 members of All Souls gathered for dinner. There was a simple symbolic communion service that resembled the communion service of neither church. It was another step in the church's program of favoring integration rather than Black Power.

The church was represented by ten persons at the General Assembly held in late June in Seattle, Washington. Dr. Kring was unable to attend as Mrs. Kring's father who was living with them, was critically ill, and passed away in September. Services for Stewart G. Mackay were held at the church on October 14, 1970. At this session of the General Assembly, it was indicated by the reports that sanity had seemingly returned to the affairs of the denomination. After the riotous meetings in 1968 at Cleveland and the 1969 meeting in Boston, this was good news. All was quiet and orderly. The assembly policed itself. The denomination was facing bankruptcy partly because of the Black Power money grants, and this year the assembly refused to grant the $250,000 to the Black Affairs Council. Dr. Kring wrote in the church calendar;

The denomination in the estimation of many has changed its course, turned the corner. As they say in Alcoholics Anonymous, you must get to the place where you can only go up before you are cured. The Association has been in that position, and now we can go up again.(20)

On Saturday May 22, 85 members of All Souls were the guests of All Souls Episcopal Church at their camp in the Catskill Mountains near Parksville. The members of the two churches were divided among the six buses. A wonderful picnic lunch was prepared by the Episcopalians, and was enjoyed with the members of the Harlem church.

It is interesting twenty years later to see if the text of Dr. Kring's sermon, "You will know them by their fruits," really came true. The Black Bonds that many churches bought with their in vested funds as a result of this enthusiasm were paid back at about half of their dollar value. The movement died a natural death after all of the money had been spent, and many ministers later expressed the opinion that they had been led astray by a false idealism that really was a wolf in sheep's clothing.

Educational Concerns

Walter Kring felt very deeply that there ought to be a serious adult educational program within the church, that members ought to have available for them lectures and discussions in which they could go into far more depth than the usual Sunday morning sermon.

The Lenten Lectures

As one of his first steps when he came to All Souls, Mr. Kring inaugurated a regular series of Lenten Lectures. These were educational in nature and over the years became a strong feature of the church's program. In 1956 Dr. Kring discussed great religious leaders, including Buddha, Lao Tze, Akhenaten, and Jesus among others. In 1959, Jesus was the general subject of the lectures and two important books about him were reviewed. The next year he addressed the subject of American Religion, looking at it through the eyes of the New England Puritans, Joseph Smith, Mary Baker Eddy, and others. In 1963, "American Philosophies of Religion" were discussed in the personalities and works of such thinkers as Jonathan Edwards, William Ellery Channing, Theodore Parker, and Rufus Jones. The next year he discussed "The Background of Christianity." In 1965 he considered the general subject of "Mysticism." And

the next year his topic was "Great Books on World Religions."
In 1967 "'Religions of the Middle East" were discussed, and in
1969 the congregation heard lectures about "Five Modern Religious Prophets," including Teilhard de Chardin, Aldous Huxley,
and Karl Barth. In 1970 he discussed "Mythology" and in 1972
the general subject was "How the Bible Came to Be the Bible."
In later years he discussed "Six Concerns of Comparative Religion" and "Mysticism, Meditation, and the Spiritual Life."

As can be seen, these Lenten Lectures covered a wide range
of religious subjects, of interest to any rational person. They required a great deal of preparation on Dr. Kring's part in addition
to his regular sermonizing and his church duties in general. But it
should not be forgotten, that these were not his only lecturing assignments. In October 1955, he began a course for members of the
congregation called "The Greatest Book." This discussion group
followed a format which had been highly successful in Worcester. These sessions were well attended, and this kind of discussion group became one of the most important feeding grounds for
membership in the church.

Course on Unitarianism

Dr. Kring also regularly gave a course of four lectures on
"Unitarianism" every fall and spring as preparation for church
membership. Many persons also came to to these lectures who
had no intention of becoming members. Dr. Kring gave these lectures during all of his 23 years at All Souls, the series as six times,
and 1250 persons joined the church during those years.

Winter Lecture Series

A series of fall and winter lectures was also given for many
years. These reached into other areas of interest. One year the subject was "The Existentialists." Another year it dealt with "Oriental

Religions," "Some Christian Heresies" were conducted in 1968. Later the Winter Lecture Series changed its form somewhat and became a lecture and discussion series. The general subject was "The Nature of Religion," and the individual topics were "Definitions of Religion," Religion and Mythology," "Religion and Theology," Religious Commitment" and "Religion and Social Change." This gives an idea of the wide range of subjects included in these popular lecture series.

The All Souls Lecture Series

In 1957, a Spring series of lectures was begun. This was called the "All Souls Lectures." This series brought many famous persons and distinguished educators to the church to consider a wide variety of topics. A sampling of the topics and speakers shows how varied and educational this series was.

In May, 1957, Mr. Kring arranged a series of lectures on "the Dead Sea Scrolls" by some of the experts in the field. The lectuers were given by Dr. James Muilenberg of Union Theological Seminary, Theodore H. Gaster of Columbia University, Dr. A. Powell Davies, minister of All Souls Unitarian Church in Washington, D.C., and Dr. Duncan Howlett, minister of the First Church in Boston. In June, the four lecturers and Mr. Kring broadcast a series of interviews on a coast to coast radio network on NBC called "Faith in Action."

In 1958 two speakers covered the field of "The Dead Sea Scrolls" in four lectures by Dr. E. A. Speiser of the University of Pennsylvania and Dr. Frank M. Cross, Jr. of Harvard University. In 1959, Dr. Harlow Shapley, Kirtley Mather, and Brand Blanshard were heard. Another year the topic was "Current American Philosophies of Religion," and invited speakers included Erwin Goodenough from Yale, Richard Niebuhr from Harvard, Julius Seelye Bixler from Colby, and Paul Tillich from Harvard. This important lecture series continued until 1968 when inflation in the country rose to double digits, and the series became a casualty of a tight budget. But the strong emphasis of this ministry on education is shown by these various lectures and discussion groups that Dr. Kring organized, promoted, and most often, led.

The Sunday School or Church School

The church school, often called the Sunday School, had for many years been an important part of the educational program at All Souls. When the Second World War ended many young families were living in the vicinity of the church. Many of them were looking for a church school for their children which taught things about God, the Bible, and other religious matters which they could believe and which made sense to them. Before Mr. Kring came to all Souls, Suzanna Wilder (later Suzanna Wilder Heinz) had built up the Sunday school in attendance and in depth of program. She resigned in 1960 after eight years service to take up similar duties at the North Shore Unitarian Church at Plandome on Long Island.

Mrs. Heinz was succeeded by Mary Leonard, a member of the church, who had worked for the J. Walter Thompson advertising agency. She carried on the work for four years until 1965 when she married John Young, a member of the church, and moved to the Midwest. She was replaced by Mrs. Edward O. Haskell, Jr., who had formerly taught at Mount Holyoke College. She in turn was succeeded by Rev. Lawrence Beebe, a graduate of Starr King School for the Ministry, who had been minister of education at several Unitarian Churches. He remained for eight years to be succeeded by Mrs. Maxine Beshers, a very active member of the church, and then by Mary-Ella Zippel, who is now Director of Religious Education Emerita. The church was fortunate to have had persons of this caliber directing the work of the Sunday School over the years.

Attendance waxed and waned over the years essentially due to the changing population of the East Side of Manhattan. In 1958 the school enrolled 190 children. In 1970 the enrollment was 176, and this size has remained fairly constant over the years.

The All Souls School: The Playground on the Roof. Photo:
George E. Joseph.

The All Souls School: Interior of one of the classrooms. Photo: George E. Joseph.

Emphasis in the teaching in the school has been an under standing not only of Unitarian Universalism but of other American and world religions. For example, in the fall of 1966, Mary Sage Mackay become the teacher of the high school group which prospered greatly and grew which prospered greatly and grew to several dozen young people, who in addition to learning about Hinduism and other religions in depth also formed a social club. They brought their friend to swell the size of the group. Mary-Ella Zippel taught the junior high group at this time, and took over the high school group later. Some of the teachers were paid a small stipend and some were volunteers.

As we look back in hindsight on that period it comes as a shock that many young people brought up with this kind of a liberal church school did not remain members of Unitarian churches in later life. Denominationally, much of that generation was, at least lost to Unitarianism. Of course, the whole emphasis in the church schools across the country was not to make Unitarians but to teach young people to think. Perhaps the teachings had too much emphasis upon other religions and the ideal of non-sectarianism which resulted in "non-sectarian nothing." But the educational level of the All Souls Church school, was always and continues to be, on a high level, and many people are attracted to the church because of the religious education program.

The All Souls Players

Another and different kind of educational outreach was the formation of a dramatic group, the All Souls Players. The first production of what was to become later to become The All Souls Players was given in April, 1963, to help the building fund. The production was called "Spring in Manhattan" and it included much original music and skits, and was repeated three times. More than a hundred members and friends of the church were involved in the various parts of the production. After the successful "Spring in Manhattan" performances, there was a move to permanently organize a players' group. On September 20, 1963, the All Souls Players had a variety program in Fellowship Hall and people were invited to become members of the group.

In 1964, the All Souls Players presented the successful Broadway musical "Fiorello" on four successive evenings in the middle of April. In 1965 they successfully tackled "The Pajama Game," another Broadway musical. "The Bells Are Ringing" was their choice for the next year. In 1967 they presented "archie and mehitabel" by James Thurber. In the fall of 1970 they presented a serious play "Caligula" by Albert Camus. In 1972 their Spring musical was "Gypsy." They gave a special performance for members of the All Souls Episcopal Church, who used all of their 200 tickets. There were another 100 tickets available for All Souls members. In 1975 "Can-Can" was their featured presentation, and in 1976 they offered George Bernard Shaw's "Saint Joan." In 1978, at the suggestion of the minister, the All Souls Players presented "Moby Dick - Rehearsed" by Orson Welles, adapted from the Herman Melville classic, and Dr. Kring before each performance spoke about Melville's relationship to All Souls Church.

The All Souls Opera Company

Another interesting musical happening at the church was the formation in 1974 of the All Souls Opera Company. It was begun by one of the members of the church, Trudy Meehan, and several other people intensely interested in opera. There was a recruitment of singers of professional status who needed experience and a chance to prove their mettle in opera. This was one of the chief purposes in founding the company. The first opera, "La Boheme," by Giacomo Puccini, was presented on February 1 and 2 in Fellowship Hall. It was well done, but New Yorkers evidently wanted to go to the Metropolitan Opera, and if not that, then the New York City Opera. In spite of highly-rated performances, attendance was always a problem, and the company always showed a financial loss, even though the lead singers were paid a "token pittance."

Later that year, on April 26 and 27, the opera company presented Puccini's "Madame Butterfly," again a superb production.

In its second season The All Souls Opera Company presented Wolfgang Amadeus Mozart's comic opera "Cosi Fan Tutte." They presented it twice in Italian and twice in English, a rather unusual presentation.

In February, 1976, after a production of Rossini's "LaCenerentola," because there were no "angels" to underwrite the company, it went into temporary and then permanent hibernation. It was a good thing that didn't work. The operas were well done, but they didn't present well known stars, and could not compete for patrons and ticket sales with the great opera companies in New York.

Building Changes

During the quarter century of Dr. Kring's stewardship many repairs and improvements were made to the physical plant of All Souls. In 1959, the rooms off Fellowship Hall and the old movie projection room were redecorated for use of the Sunday School. By 1961, the need for more space was evident.

A special congregational meeting was held on December 4, 1961, which considered two subjects: 1. Whether to build an addition to Wiggin House, and 2. Whether to conduct a campaign for funds to erect such a building with a goal of $150,000. This vote climaxed a long period of study, for it was deemed improvident to build an addition to Wiggin House which would only be used on Sunday mornings for the church school. It soon became apparent that a nursery and kindergarten conducted during the daytime on week days would provide a full use of the building, and there was a real need in the community for such a school. The John Lindsley Fund had agreed to match up to $150,000 for this purpose. Mr. Thayer Lindsley was a member of the church, and Dr. Kring was acting as the executive trustee for the fund. When the campaign was in full stride, it soon became apparent that the sum was too much to raise, so the Lindsley Fund agreed to increase their match to two for one.

In 1962, Mrs. Frederick Wappler, chairman of the building campaign, announced that $60,000 had already been pledged. The people of All Souls, having been burned in their last building project by the Great Depression were not about to start a building project until they had all of the money pledged.

The Day School

A special meeting of the congregation was called for April 9 to act upon two recommendations of the board of trustees. 1. The acquisition of an apartment in a building adjoining the church edifice for office space, and 2. The establishment of a day school for children of nursery and kindergarten age in the enlarged Wiggin House. The congregation approved both items.

These items did not come as a surprise to anyone. There had been long discussions in committees and among the members about the advisability of starting a nursery school, and while Wiggin House was being enlarged it was necessary to find some additional office space. An apartment had become vacant on the ground floor of the apartment house just to the east of the church on 80th Street, and it was possible to cut a doorway through the back wall of the church, thus connecting the two buildings. It was purchased on what now seem rather reasonable terms. It was pointed out that the building campaign for $100,000 ought to be completed as soon as possible so that work could be started on the enlarging of Wiggin House.

The campaign was helped considerably when Lee Adams, a member of the church who had written the lyrics to "Bye Bye Birdie," a very successful Broadway musical, donated to the church one-fourth of his residual rights to the production. This meant that every time that a theatre group did "Bye Bye Birdie" the church received a commission. Since this musical has a lot of young people in it, it has been very popular through the years, and the church has continued to profit handsomely from this generous gift.

In June 1964, the bids for the new addition to Wiggin House were received from six contractors. All of them were in excess of the estimated cost of $300,000 for the addition. The board called a meeting of the congregation on June 8 to vote on the proposition of taking $50,000 out of capital funds to assure that the building could be built. The congregation approved.(21)

The members of the congregation were able to see the interior of the enlarged Wiggin House for the first time on October 17, 1965. One headmaster spoke of the new school building as "the finest pre-school structure in the city." There was no formal dedication ceremony as the building had been dedicated in 1954. The All Souls School had opened on September 23, 1965, with a director, a secretary-bookeeper, six full-time teachers and six part-time teachers. with full use in the mornings and partial use in the afternoons.

In 1964, Miss Margaret Fitchen was chosen as head of the new day school. She had had a rich experience of 34 years when she came to All Souls with a strong endorsement by leaders in the field of early childhood education. Other plans for the day school indicated that the tuition would probably be between $500 and $600, and that children of church members would be given preference in admission. Over the years this did not prove to necessary because fully 95% of the students were not children of church members. The day school committee wanted to emphasize that the school was conceived as a service to the community. The day school committee consisted of Dr. Arne Groningsater, a teacher at Horace Mann School, chairman, Miss Martha Allen, executive director of the Campfire Girls of America, E. Eugene Grossman, Gunnar A Johnansson, a high school teacher, Dr. Kring, William B. Nichols, John R. Petty, Miss Marie Russo, a school teacher, and Mrs. M. Lauck Walton, with Miss Alice Taggart, the parish assistant, as an ex-officio member.(22)

On April 23, 1965, the All Souls School was chartered by the New York State Board of Regents, and the board of trustees of the school appointed by the church board became the first board of trustees of the school. Miss Fitchen stated at the time of the granting of the charter that there were already 85 children of nursery and kindergarten age enrolled for the Fall term. The school continues active to this day.

Refurbishing of Fellowship Hall

The church during the early part of 1968 was the recipient of $500,000 from the John Lindsley Fund. It was for endowment purposes, and came to All Souls as the capital of the Lindsley Fund was being dispersed. This new endowment had not been anticipated when the 1968 budget had been made, so it was decided to use the income during the year for the renovation of Fellowship Hall which was once described as "a glorified basement."

The church hired an architect, a new floor was put down, an acoustical ceiling installed, a sound-enhancing wall was erected at the rear of the hall. The architect was in Dr. Kring's office one day discussing the preliminary planning, and he noticed some colored glass windows which had been crafted by Dr. Kring. He said that because of the great cost he would not normally advise colored glass windows for Fellowship Hall. But since he assumed the minister would be willing to contribute his services for designing and building the windows, he thought that by making a dozen large panels of glass with lighting behind them Fellowship Hall would look a lot less like a basement.

Dr. Kring submitted several designs to the architect, and one which was rather modern was chosen. The finest European glass was used, and mosaics of random small pieces of glass were alternated with panels of a single color. The whole was put together in aluminum frames with flexible epoxy glue, and with fluorescent lights behind the glass. There are some 10,000 individual pieces of glass in the "windows." They have held up perfectly. With all of these improvements, Fellowship Hall was transformed.

Refurbished Fellowship Hall during the Coffee Hour. Photo: George E. Joseph.

The extensive remodeling of Fellowship Hall had been delayed by a painter's strike. But at the end of December, 1968, the president of the board of trustees, Edward N. Costikyan, was able to report to the congregation that the work was now finished. In describing the new windows, he said;

> *The result of all this work, we believe, is exciting and aesthetically pleasing. The scale of the room is much more grand. . . We believe that in these windows Dr. Kring has created beauty which will last as long as the church.(23)*

Other changes were made in the sanctuary. The Austin organ in the church had been dedicated on October 2, 1932, a gift of members of the von Bernuth family. Since that time only routine maintenance had been done on the organ. Now it needed a complete overhaul brought on by years of wear and the disintegration of the leather pads. The Austin Company of Hartford, Connecticut, the original builders, made the low bid. The John Lindsley Fund gave $35,000, and the church used $15,000 of capital funds to make the work possible. It was hoped that the organ could be enlarged, but it never was. This is the organ that has recently been removed from the church to make way for the new organ in memory of John and Eleanor French.

On November 26, 1972, a temporary pulpit was installed in the church. There had been complaints for many years that the acoustics of the church were excellent for music but bad for speaking. The congregation tended to hear the echo of each word in addition to hearing the words directly. Many things had been tried including the installation of a carpet over the slate floor of the church. This new experiment placed a pulpit very close to the front of the chancel toward the north side of the church. It proved to make the words of the minister much easier to hear, and it is still in place.

Gifts to the Church

Over the years parishioners and friends of All Souls have been very generous and supportive of its work with gifts. This was as true during Dr. Kring's tenure as it has been in the years before and since.

It was announced at the communion service on January 6, 1957, that Mrs. Laurance Neale had given two communion plates to the church in memory of Alice Kent Neale and Laurance Irving Neale.

At the annual meeting held on January 15, 1957, the congregation heard for the first time the details of a recent gift which had come to the church. By the wills of Mrs. Carrie von Bernuth Foot and her half sister, Miss Louise Emily von Bernuth, the church received bequests of cash and securities in excess of $846,000. These bequests originated from a long and devoted association of the Foot and von Bernuth families with All Souls Church. Frederick Augustus von Bernuth was the father of the two bene factors. He joined the church in 1885. The rest of the family signed the membership book in 1904. The wills had been held in trust for surviving members of the family. The last member had died in the summer of 1956, and the funds had come immediately into the endowment funds of All Souls Church.

"Both Mrs. Foot and Miss von Bernuth were gracious, unostentatious women, who through years of church interest had undoubtedly determined, possibly in concert, that their beloved church needed a permanent endowment of significant proportions."(24) They had no idea that when the church received the funds it would be such a large amount, as it had been invested wisely over the years and the principle of the fund had grown sizably. It was voted to erect a tablet in memory of Carrie von Bernuth Foot and Louise Emily von Bernuth, and the choir henceforth was to be designated as "The Foot von Bernuth Memorial Choir." In 1956, Miss Maud Perry Mills also left the church $50,000 in her will, Carl and Marian Eckstron $10,000, and Miss Neale $1,000. Never had the church received so much support from its deceased members. The invested funds were quadrupled in 1956.

A plaque in memory of Rev. Dr. Laurance Irving Neale, was unveiled at the morning service on Sunday November 10, 1957. The plaque is on the south wall of the sanctuary. The unveiling of the plaque honoring Dr. Neale was part of the morning service which was an observance of the 25th anniversary of the dedication of the present building.

On Sunday May 17, 1959, the Laurance Irving Neale Library was dedicated. It is a collection of books dealing with religion and the Unitarian faith, and was given by the church to honor Dr. Neale. Charles Sherover, the head of the library committee, gave the keys to Samuel M. Lane, the chairman of the board of trustees.

A new communion service of sterling silver was presented to the church in 1958 by Dr. and Mrs. Alfred H. Ehrenclou in memory of Dr. Minot Simons. Increased attendance at the communion service had made it necessary to increase the four sets to six sets. The church was also the recipient the same year of two new silver collection plates, the gift of Mrs. Edward R. Gay and Mrs. Edgar J. Brower in memory of Alexander Draper, Caroline Louise Scott, and Enoch Armitage.

In 1961, it was reported that a set of English Whitechapel handbells had been the gift of the organist, William Henry Brewster. They were to be used occasionally at the morning service. At the annual meeting on January 16, William Brewster's twenty-five-year service as organist and choirmaster, was recognized and celebrated. Dr. Kring on behalf of the church presented Mr. Brewster with a plaque in commemoration of his service to the church.

In early 1969, a new bronze work of art was added to the Memorial Garden. It featured three girls carrying balloons. The bronze, located on the West wall of the Chapel, was sculpted by Euphemia Glover, and was cast across from the church on Eightieth Street at the foundry of Harold Castor. Dr. Kring had seen a small version of this work of art at one of the shows of the Artist Craftsmen of New York, and after securing a gift which made it possible, he asked Mrs. Glover to make the larger sculpture.

"The mood of the statue is thoroughly in keeping with the philosophy of the Memorial Garden. The garden was given and endowed by Mr. and Mrs. Samuel Ordway in 1955 as a memorial to two of their children who died in their infancy. The garden is a happy spot in the midst of our big city, and the girls with their balloons depict in a real way the happy spirit of childhood. The children represent the three major races of the world and thus signify the entire family of man and the brotherhood that ought to exist between all people."(25)

Mr. Costikyan the same year announced the new endowment of $500,000 from the John Lindsley Fund. He stated that it was hoped that the income from this new fund could be used for special purposes, and with this in mind he pointed out that with the new gift, the annual gift of $11,000 from the Lindsley Fund to the church would cease, and that somehow the annual appeal had to make up that amount.

During the 150th Anniversary in 1969 it had become apparent to many members of the church that there were two significant omissions honoring the former ministers of the church. There was no plaque in honor of William Ellery Channing, who had been the spiritual founder of the church, and Charles Theodore Christian Follen, who had not been acceptable to the congregation after William Ware had resigned. He served the church as acting minister from 1836-1838. Arthur Holden designed the two plaques, an appeal for money for this purpose went out to the congregation, and the two plaques were installed on the south wall of the sanctuary.

Early in the year 1972 the sexton of the church, Rafael Torres, found a charcoal drawing of Henry Whitney Bellows in one of the tower storerooms. Some research was done on the artist, George Rufus Boynton, and it was determined that the sketch was probably done after Bellows' death from a photograph. It now hangs in the Bellows Room of the church.

In November 1977, it was announced that the church was the

recipient of a treasured gift from a direct descendent of Henry Ware, Jr, who in the early days of the church had helped the congregation to endure. Mr. Malcolm Ware of Brookline, Massachusetts, presented to the church a sterling silver lavabo which had been presented to William Ware, the first minister of All Souls in 1833. A lavabo was used by the early ministers to wash their hands before the communion service when the elements were passed to the communicants by the minister.

Mr. Malcolm Ware also made the church a very significant gift of a copy of a portrait of Mary Ware (Mrs. William Ware). The original was a companion picture to the portrait of Mr. Ware by James Frothingham in the Ware Room, and was painted by the same artist. Mr. Ware had intended to give the original to the church, but when he sent it to be cleaned at the Boston Museum of Fine Arts, they expressed a keen interest in the picture for their collection as being one of the finest portraits of the period.

When Dr. Kring went to visit Mr. Ware in Brookline, Mr. Ware asked him if there was good "security" for valuable portraits at All Souls. Dr. Kring had to admit that there wasn't, as there had been several break-ins at the church. Would All Souls be interested in a copy? The answer was "Yes, that will serve our purposes in honoring Mrs. Ware just as well as the original." So the Boston Museum set about getting a copy made.

It was at this time that Edwin Land, famous inventor and the founder of the Polaroid Corporation, was experimenting with a large camera to make fine full-size reproduction of great works of art. He had developed a new process in which one could not very readily tell the difference between the original and the copy unless one got very close to the copy. It just so happened that the portrait of Mrs. Ware was only the third done by Mr. Land. So All Souls got not just a portrait of Mrs. Ware but one of the earliest portraits ever done with the new technique.

Among Ourselves

In a quarter of a century many changes come into the lives of the members of a church.

Early in Dr. Kring's ministry the All Souls church family suffered two serious losses in the almost immediate future. Miss Alice Neale, Dr. Neale's sister, much beloved of the congregation, died on January 4, 1956. She had been chairman and treasurer of the All Souls Red Cross unit for many years, chairman of the flower committee for as long as anyone could remember, and president of the New York Fruit and Flower Mission.

Nothing shook up the new minister more than the death of Dr. Neale in April 1956. Mr. Kring had been counting on Dr. Neale's help and advice as he began his ministry. Now he would have to carry on without this wise fraternal assistance. Dr. Neale had also planned to write the history of All Souls in his retirement, but he became ill so shortly after he retired that he never began the project.

Funeral services were held on February 9, 1957, for Mark Walton Maclay, the prominent admiralty lawyer who had formerly been president of the board of trustees, and constantly active in the church. His services over the years and his loyalty to the church, particularly during the hard times, had been outstanding. A happier event was the announcement in 1962 that Spencer Lavan, who grew up in All Souls, had been ordained into the Unitarian ministry. He had attended Crane Theological School at Tufts University, and was now the minister of the Unitarian Church in Charleston, South Carolina. At present, he is the dean of Meadville Lombard Theological School in Chicago.

In May, 1964, the board of trustees passed a resolution concerning the service to the church by Frederick W. Ecker, the former president of the Metropolitan Life Insurance Company, who had recently died. He had served in many distinguished positions in the church. Special mention was made of:

His sage advice in financial matters in the depression

years and the very trying days of the Second World War
when the church was in financial difficulties before the
"Burn the Mortgage Campaign" brought us from the de-
spondency of debt, the church might very well not have
survived financially to bring a religious message to the
New York Community.(26)

On Thursday, October 5, 1967, a memorial service was held for Samuel M. Lane. The previous February, Mr. Lane, who was an avid sailor, had been scheduled to take a fifty-foot sailing yacht from Massachusetts to Bermuda. The other two sailors backed out at the last moment, but Samuel Lane decided to sail alone during the winter storms. He was never heard from again, and by October it was apparent that he was not any longer to be listed as "missing," but that he had drowned. He had contributed much to the church through many years. A prominent lawyer, and the head of his firm, Casey, Lane and Mittendorf, he was sorely missed. The trustees adopted a resolution of appreciation for what he had done for the church over the years

The trustees also adopted a resolution of appreciation for the services of William B. Nichols who had passed away on September 9, 1967. Mr. Nichol's service to the church extended over many years. He had been a member of the board in 1922 when Dr. William Lawrence Sullivan had proposed a series of great preachers rather than a preaching minister for All Souls. Mr. Nichols had been one of the trustees who had resigned in protest. Recently he had served as the president of the board of trustees.

On December 29, 1967, Charles Chester Lane died. He had been active in the church for many years and he had held almost all of the offices. A successful business man in his own right, the assistant business manager of The New York Times, he was a conservative Unitarian who believed that on the national scene many things were happening to equate liberal religion with liberal politics and liberal social theory, which he opposed. But so far as the welfare of All Souls was concerned he is one of those without whom the church would have foundered in its financial woes.

On January 23, 1973 the annual meeting as usual was held in Fellowship Hall. After dinner a few minutes was taken from the business for all to listen to the President announce that a "Cease Fire" had been signed to end the Vietnam conflict. All Souls had a casualty in that war, and Dr. Kring spoke about Steven Elbert after the President's announcement. Steve Elbert began attending All Souls Sunday School when he was ten years of age. He was elected president of the young people's group, joined the church, and was active in young people's district and national Unitarian Universalist groups. After graduation from City College in 1965, he had worked with a VISTA group in Hartford, Connecticut. The Vietnam draft caught up with him in the summer of 1967. He applied for the medical corps, and was trained as a medic. He received the Bronze Star, the Purple Heart, and the Good Conduct Medal. Unfortunately, these were awarded posthumously, for he was killed on April 17, 1968, a little more than three months after he arrived in Vietnam.

Dr. Kring wrote in the church calendar for October 2, 1977, about the passing of an era. Eric H. Ganley had died at the age of eighty on September 14. Mrs. Ganley, who was very active in the church, had died earlier in the year. They were almost the last of an amazing and talented group of Jewish refugees who fled from Adolph Hitler in the late 1930's and early 1940's. When they came to the United States, many of them looked around for a religion which they could join in good conscience. Many joined All Souls. By 1977 there were very few of these people left. The Ganley's escaped the madman Hitler. At All Souls Church they found a new human dignity which exalted them rather than destroyed them. Actually, today there is still one person left in the church who as a child went through the horrors of a Nazi concentration camp.(27)

At the General Assembly of the Unitarian Universalist Association during the last week in June, Sandra Mitchell Caron, long an All Souls member, was elected the moderator of the Association. She received a total of 1,043 votes compared to the 813 votes received by William Holway of Tulsa, Oklahoma. Dr. Paul Carnes was elected president of the Association, receiving 1,099 votes to the 938 for Dr. Jack Mendelssohn. Traditionally, the moderator was a lay person and a volunteer, and the president had always been a minister, and was a full-time employee. During the next eight years that Sandra Caron served as moderator she enlarged the scope of the position, and it almost seemed at times as if it were a full-time position.

The duties of the Moderator are arduous. He or she must visit many churches, making numerous public appearances, preside at meetings of the board of trustees and at the General Assembly. The members of the church were proud that one of their own had been elected to such a high post in the denomination, and they were pleased when four years later she was elected for a second term so that she served the limit of two full four-year terms.

Personal Remembrances

During this near quarter of a century there were some personal events in Dr. Kring's life which had some impact on the church life.

On July 19, 1962, Dr. Kring returned from his vacation in Massachusetts to perform a very interesting and significant wed ding ceremony, the marriage of Paul Gray Hoffman, who had been the director of the European Recovery Program (The Marshall Plan) among other achievements, and Anna M. Rosenberg, who had been the Assistant Secretary of Defense under President Truman. Dr. Kring said that it was the only time that he had married two people whose Who's Who in America biographies read something like this; "Honorary degrees from Harvard, Yale, Princeton, and many other universities."

At a ceremony held on May 21, 1970, Dr. Kring was awarded a silver medal by the American Museum of Natural History for his services to the museum. He had already been made an honorary life member of the museum. These services had been in connection with a large gift from the John Lindsley Fund which donated a new hall of geology at the museum. The medal had been struck for the 100th anniversary of the museum. Nine such medals in gold were awarded to the Apollo 10 astronauts and six prominent scientists. Three silver medals had been previously awarded. Dr. Kring, as the executive trustee of the John Lindsley Fund, had worked as a representative of Thayer Lindsley for several years with the museum staff in setting up the John Lindsley Hall of Geology at the museum.

On Tuesday, January 20, 1969, at the 151st annual meeting, Edward N. Costikyan, as moderator, announced that Dr. Kring. had been elected president of the Spence Chapin Adoption Service for a two-year term. Spence Chapin was one of the largest adoption services on the East Coast, and one of its programs started at the request of the city, was to find foster homes for newly born infants who could not be let out of the hospitals because they had no homes. When Dr. Kring became the president of Spence Chapin he had to sign legal papers that as president made him the legal guardian of 1,100 foster children, all of them black.

Dr. Kring wrote in the calendar for January 16, 1972, that he was just about to complete his two-year term as the president of the Spence Chapin Adoption Service. He had taken over the presidency from one of the members of All Souls Church, Mrs. Alice Dowling, who had died just as her term ended. It had been the most difficult two years in the history of the agency. There had been the successful completion of two protracted eye-catching and news-making legal struggles in the New York Superior Court. In the Di Martino case, the couple fled New York state with their adopted child to escape the jurisdiction of the courts. In the Polk case a Jewish foster mother fell in love with a little Chinese girl and she refused to let the agency have the child when the agency had arranged for her mother to take her home. The child was finally rescued and given to its mother. But the foster mother sued the agency for some millions of dollars. The judge finally closed the case forever and no damages were awarded. Dr. Kring wrote that working with a wonderful board of directors and a completely inter-racial staff of 125 persons at Spence Chapin had been one of the best experiences of his life. He now gave up his legal responsibility of being the "father" of the 1,100 black children in the foster homes managed by the agency.

On March 28, 1974, Dr. Kring conducted funeral services for Peter Revson, the son of the head of the Revlon Company and a well-known racing driver who was killed in an accident in South Africa, while he was testing his car. The church was packed, and Dr. Kring said that he believed that it was the first time that a picture of the interior of a church had ever made the sports page of *The New York Times*. Why the service was held at All Souls is still a mystery except that Peter Revson had no church or synagogue connections. Dr. Kring also had to spend some time keeping the former "Miss Universe" away from the reporters and photographers. Mr. Revson and she had been seeing each other a great deal, and Dr. Kring said it was probably the first and last time that he could hide a "Miss Universe" in his study.

On May 17, 1977, Dr. Kring was asked to conduct a memorial service in the church for the famous movie start Joan Crawford.Miss Crawford was not a Unitarian. In fact she was a Christian Scientist, which sect does not believe either in death or in funerals. But Miss Crawford had been married to the chairman of the board of the Pepsi Corporation, and she had been a member of the board since her husbands' death. So Dr. Kring was put in the position of trying to arrange a memorial service with the public relations department of the Pepsi Corporation, and the distraught adopted daughter, Christina Crawford, who had just been informed that her mother's will had disinherited her. But the memorial service did take place with an overflowing crowd. Christina's later revelations about child abuse in her book about her up-bringing by her mother as the daughter of a Hollywood movie star shocked many people.

A Surprise Resignation

On Sunday morning, June 13, 1976, Dr. Kring made an announcement from the pulpit that surprised everyone except the members of the board of trustees who had discussed the matter for several months. He said in part:

> *This is the last Sunday in the church year, and when we return in the fall I will have completed twenty-one years as your minister, next to the forty-three-year tenure of Henry Bellows the second longest pastorate in the history of our church.*
>
> *After much soul searching I have shared with the board of trustees, and I now share with you, my desire to retire from the ministry of this church on September 1, 1978 - two years from now. I have been discussing this possibility with the board of trustees, and it now appears that we will be able to work out the details of such an early retirement.*
>
> *One of the reasons that I am making this announcement two years before actual retirement it that it takes a congregation in a church as important as this one a long time to assess themselves, to think about the direction they want this institution to move in the future, and to select an energetic younger man to offer leadership to this congregation. My announcement at this time will make it possible for you plan adequately and not hurriedly.*

On July 30 Dr. Kring wrote a letter to all of the members of the congregation explaining his decision in a little more detail as it was evident that many did not understand his abrupt resignation. Some thought that the minister was being forced out, which was not the case. Dr. Kring wrote that he was looking forward very much to finishing the biography of Henry Bellows and making some pottery when the two-year period of searching for a new minister was completed and a successor had been elected.

A Search Begins Anew

A special congregational meeting was held after services on March 6, 1977, to elect five members to serve on a search committee to select a successor to Dr. Kring. Five members were to be chosen by the congregation, and two members were to be ap pointed by the board of trustees. The search committee as finally selected consisted of; W. Stephens Dietz, John French, Jane Levenson, Ricardo Mestres, Florence B. McKinlay, Jeanne Walton, and Bert Zippel, chairman. They set to work immediately to pre pare a questionaire about the church and the wishes of the congregation as a first preliminary step for selecting a new minister.

The board of trustees called a special congregational meet-ing to consider several issues. The first was that the congregation act on whether to ordain Jonathan Sinclair Carey to the Unitar-ian Universalist ministry. That took only a few minutes. Then the congregation heard three speakers; Dr. David Pohl of the Depart-ment of the Ministry of the Unitarian Universalist Association, Dr. Kenneth Helfant, chairman of the Plandome Church which had re-cently been through the process of calling a new minister, and Dr. Peter Samsom, the appointed settlement minister of the Metro-politan District. The church had not called a minister since 1955, twenty-two years prior to this meeting. There were many people present who had participated in that event twenty-two years ago, and they had not realized that the rules of calling a minister had changed drastically since Dr. Kring had been called.

The new plan was for the congregation to elect a search com-mittee, which they had already done. This committee in secret would narrow down a list of suggestions from headquarters, and add any candidates they desired. Then when the field had been narrowed down to perhaps six or eight, some members of the committee would visit the minister's home churches, hear them preach, and interview them. Some candidates might be brought to New York City for an interview, but they would not preach at All Souls. The search committee then would narrow its choice down to a single candidate. He or she would be asked to preach at All Souls on two consecutive Sundays. In the intervening week he or she would meet as many of the congregation as possible in a more informal manner.

After the candidating week was concluded, the congregation

would then accept or reject the selection of the search committee. According to the All Souls By-Laws, it would take a two-thirds majority to call a minister. Some of the "old timers" felt that they were being cheated in not hearing more candidates. But as David Pohl pointed out, the new rules had been drawn up not only by the association but also by the ministers association. The old system of "Serial Candidating" made it difficult for those who were not chosen in this process. The congregation finally accepted the necessity for All Souls to follow the new rules.

Some people later asked why All Souls did not follow the custom of having an interim minister for a year or more while a successor was selected. The matter was considered. But at that time it was felt that an interim minister was only necessary if the church had been through some trauma or deep problems. All Souls has always had some problems. But although it had had some difficult sailing during Dr. Kring's ministry, the church had never foundered on the rocks. In addition, the church had almost two years in which to choose a successor after Dr. Kring decided to take early retirement. This made the chances for the right choice better, and seemed to promise a peaceful and smooth transition to the new minister.

Hail and Farewell

A special service was held on Sunday morning, April 16, 1978, to honor Dr. Kring. Sandra Caron, the moderator of the Unitarian Universalist Association, and a member of All Souls, opened the service. Dr. Rhys Williams, minister of the First and Second Church in Boston, spoke a few words, as did Rev. F. Forrester Church, the minister-elect. Jonathan Carey, former student assistant at All Souls who had helped Dr. Kring with his Melville research, and who was now was doing graduate work at Yale, also spoke. Dr. Paul Carnes, the president of the Unitarian Universalist Association preached the sermon, May 19, 1978, the congregation put on a farewell dinner in Fellowship Hall for Dr. and

Mrs. Kring. After a wonderful dinner, a toast had been prepared by Arthur Holden. After assuring the gathering that he was no Bob Hope, he said in part:

I'm sure Walter has, quietly in his own way, given us much to think about. As we revolve in our minds the thought that he has stimulated, I'm convinced we will come to realize that we owe Walter Kring our everlasting gratitude for the 23 years that he has spent with us as the simple unassuming minister of All Souls.(28)

After Mr. Holden had finished his toast, Dr. Bert Zippel, the chairman of the committee that had planned the celebration, presented several gifts to Dr. Kring. The first was an original edition of *The Confidence Man* by Herman Melville, the second was a Korean decorated celadon of the Korai dynasty, and the third was a purse donated by many individuals. Bert said "this is for a trip to China." After the presentation and Dr. Kring's response, there was an evening of dancing and general celebration.

The service on Sunday morning June 11 was in honor of Dr. Kring's last Sunday in the pulpit. Florence McKinlay and Betty van Zandt read from Dr. Kring's writings. Stephens Dietz led in prayer. Words of appreciation were given by Rafael Torres, the sexton. Willard Brown and Suzan Blatz spoke for the congregation. Marianne Roffman read a letter from Mrs. Samuel M. Lane. Sally Smith spoke of Dr. Kring's work for the Unitarian Universalist Service Committee. Rev. Melvin van der Workeen brought greetings from the Unitarian Universalist United Nations Office where Dr. Kring had served as president for many years. Monona Rossol spoke for the Artist Craftsmen of New York of which society Dr. Kring had been the president for five years. Mrs. Jane Edwards, the executive director of Spence Chapin Adoption Service, spoke, as did Dr. Donald Yannella, secretary of the Melville Society, which Dr. Kring served as president the following year. Dr. Kring wrote that he was reluctant to try to preach a final sermon and had always depended upon his friends.

Thus ended almost a quarter of a century in the life of All Souls. The potter of All Souls could now concentrate on private creations.

The Ninth Minister of All Souls, Dr. F. Forrester Church.

CHAPTER 7

Realizing A Great Vision: with an Epilogue:

F. Forrester Church Becomes Ninth Minister, 1978.

If religion is our human response to the dual reality of being alive and having to die, my father (Senator Frank Church) from a very early age, was touched with natural grace. Because my father was not afraid to die, he was not afraid to live. He did not spend his life, as so many of us do, little by little until he was gone. He gave it away to others. . . Peacefully, naturally, with serenity and grace, he returned his light unto the eternal horizon. Like the day star, my father went out with the dawn.

F. Forrester Church.(1)

Son of a Senator

In choosing its ninth minister, All Souls reached high. Frank Forrester Church IV was born September 23, 1948. He spent his early years in Washington D.C. where his father for many years was a distinguished senator from Idaho, and in Idaho which was their real home. He attended Stanford University. He did not always follow in his father's footsteps.

During the late 60's, Forrest was a rebellious teenager, angry over the war in Vietnam and almost everything else that seemed to be wrong with the world. In fact, Dr. Church remembers heated arguments which he had with his father. He did not believe that anything good could come out of the establishment, including his father's heretical little corner of it. He was manning barricades and waiting for the world to end, and he believed that only a massive revolution would save society. He felt that his father was part of a compromise point of view that had brought about the (Vietnam) war. Senator Church was actually the fourth senator to come out against the war, long before it became expedient to do so.

Forrester recalls that he grew a beard and lived in the basement of the house in Idaho and wrote bad poetry, listened to the Beatles and read books about the Russian revolution. In 1968 he refused to campaign for his father who was running for re-election. He described his feelings about the war and the flag:

During the Vietnam period, when pro-war activists festooned their lapels with little American flags, my friends and I turned the flag upside down; others who shared many of our views even burned it. Yet, if, as I believe, we were acting as true patriots in opposing a war that betrayed some of the highest principles and values of our country, then we made a terrible mistake when we ceded the flag to those who, while claiming it as their own, were quite possibly desecrating it.(2)

A turning point in Forrester's life came when he graduated from Stanford University. He married his fellow student, Amy Furth, who was a class below him at Stanford. He attended the Pacific School of Religion while waiting for his wife to graduate from Stanford. They both planned to enter the Peace Corps.

But then unexpectedly President Nixon announced that henceforth Peace Corps volunteers would be eligible for the army draft. Forrester was vehemently opposed to the war, and if drafted, he planned to file for the status of a conscientious objector. He was pulled between a career in law or academia. He opted to go to Harvard Divinity School. Also divinity students were exempt from the draft.

Both Forrester and Amy graduated from Harvard Divinity

School in 1974. Amy became acting dean of students while Forrester switched to a doctoral program in church history. His career
now gave every indication that he would end up as a professor.
His field of specialty was first and second century Gnosticism,
about as arcane a subject as one could choose. His thesis was
about the newly discovered Gospel of Thomas, one of the Nag
Hamadi documents found in upper Egypt in 1947, and he had to
learn to read the Coptic language in order to write his dissertation.

Invited to All Souls

Meanwhile he worked for several years as a student assistant
at the First and Second Church in Boston under its pastor, Rev. Dr.
Rhys Williams. Here he began to see how a church operated. He
preached a few times at the church and a few times elsewhere. He
was ordained at the First and Second Church in 1975.

When he was invited by Dr. Kring to preach at the summer services in 1977, the newly formed search committee was
alerted and several members heard him preach on August 28.
They were impressed. Several members pushed hard to see that
Mr. Church was given an invitation to come to All Souls to succeed Dr. Kring. When it became obvious that the committee was
unanimous in its choice, they invited Mr. Church to come to
New York City for an interview.

Even when he accepted the invitation to come to New York
City as a candidate he still believed that he would turn down the
church. But his interview showed him the kind of a church that
All Souls was, and he quickly changed his mind. He wrote about
that interview:

*Halfway through the interview, I discovered - the most
amazing thing - my calling. I'll even use the old language.
I was called. Here were these seven, wonderful, bright,
diverse people, all of whom were clearly devoted to this
community of faith and service. What possessed them to
choose me, I'll never fully understand, but my life began*

anew that September ten years ago when I entered into the
ministry that they and you entrusted me with.(3)

He hurriedly finished up his thesis so that he received his
Ph.D. in June from Harvard University.

Why would a prestigious New York City church like All Souls
take such a gamble on a man who had never had a pastorate and
who was headed for the teaching profession? Forrester Church
said in a sermon "How My Mind Has Changed," which he delivered on the occasion of his tenth anniversary as minister of All
Souls: "I didn't really begin practicing ministry until I came to
All Souls ten years ago this month."(4) What the committee at
All Souls saw in F. Forrester Church was his potential to be a
truly great minister and a leader of the church. What he lacked
in experience, they believed he possessed in ability. He was very
good with people. Even though all of his adult life had been in
educational institutions, he had somehow developed the kind of
personality that made his father famous, an ability to meet people
well and to get along with them.

But preaching Sunday after Sunday was new to him. Prior to
his coming to All Souls he had perhaps preached a dozen sermons.
Church tells the story:

The president of the congregation came in to my office one
day and said, "Forrest, you're doing a wonderful job. But
some of us were wondering whether you might consider
putting a little more time into your sermons." The problem
wasn't time. Back then I put 20 hours a week into my ser-
mons. The problem was experience. And faith."(5)

But if the 30-year-old minister had some self-doubts, the
church itself thrived under its new leadership. He tackled the
problems that existed, and if he didn't know about such things he
read about them; fund raising, for example.

Participants in the installation of Dr. Church. From left to right: Dr. Bert Zippel, Moderator, Dr. Church, and Dr. King.

Dr. F. Forrester Church was installed as the ninth minister of the Unitarian Church of All Souls on Sunday afternoon, November 12, at a 4:30P.M. service. Gathered were not only the members of the congregation and friends of Dr. Church, but also many of the ministers of the New York area, ministers of neighboring Protestant and Catholic Churches, Jewish synagogues, and many Unitarian Universalist ministers.

The service began with a processional to Beethoven's "Ode to Joy" from the Ninth Symphony. As was the custom at All Souls, one of the laity led the opening of the service, on this occasion Martha Stillman who was chairman of the worship commission.

Rev. Dr. Rhys Williams, the minister of the First and Second Church in Boston, under whom Dr. Church had served as assistant for several years, and in which church he had been ordained, read the Scripture Lesson.

The All Souls Choir sang a rendition of Psalm 86 by Gustav Holst. Sandra Caron, a member of All Souls, and the moderator of the Unitarian Universalist Association, brought greetings from the denomination. After the singing of a hymn, Maxine Beshers, the president of the board of trustees, led the congregation in the act of installation.

The congregation stood, and Mrs. Beshers said:

> *"We shall now proceed to recognize formally the relation of people and minister that exists between this Parish and Frank Forrester Church. We do this whole-heartedly because it is a consummation representing our best judgment. The results we hope for through this relationship, however, are possible only if we as a people acknowledge obligations of loyalty and cooperation. Are we ready to assume these obligations?"*

The congregation responded: "We are ready and willing to take upon ourselves these obligations, and we do solemnly promise to fulfill them in spirit and in truth to the best of our ability."

Then the moderator turned to the minister-elect and asked him if accepted his responsibilities. Dr. Church replied: "With all humility of heart but with an uplifted spirit I accept the high and holy trust which you have committed to me."

Dr. George Huntston Williams, under whom Forrest had written his doctoral thesis at Harvard, then gave the prayer of installation. Dr. Krister Stendahl, the Dean of the Harvard Divinity School, gave the charge to the minister, and Dr. Kring, now minister emeritus, gave the charge to the congregation. After the singing of "Praise to the Living God," Dr. Church gave the benediction, and everyone went downstairs to Fellowship Hall for a gala reception. Thus began formally Dr. Church's ministry at All Souls.

Some Concluding Thoughts

Of necessity, we must leave the history of All Souls in an unfinished state. History is what has happened in the past, the present is now operative and soon becomes the future. So, no one can predict the future of All Souls Church. That is in the hands of many factors including what happens in American and world history.

I will not attempt to predict the future, but I can speak of the 159 years of the past, for I have learned much in doing the research and writing this trilogy of books about our history. No one had ever read all of the papers of Henry Bellows before I set out on that four-month task. Dr. Neale, who wanted to write the history of the church, and who had participated in a great deal of making the history, could not have anticipated such a lengthy and thorough history of his dear church. Even when I was the minister of the church, it was not until I undertook to write the history that I really understood the continuity of the spirit of All Souls over all these years.

All Souls was founded in 1819 after the visit of William Ellery Channing, because a group of men, most of them from New England, wanted the kind of a free church for which Channing and the new Unitarian movement stood. They wanted to open up the old orthodoxies to reason, and they did not want to establish a new liberal orthodoxy.

There has been over the years a constant striving to find new meaning for liberals in religious thinking. Liberals tend to degenerate their thinking like others, into stereotypes. Liberals tend to become as set in their doctrines as the orthodox. But this has not been particularly true of the ministers of All Souls, all nine of them, plus Charles Theodore Christian Pollen, the acting minister from 1836-1838. It is true that in many ways the ministers represented some of the progressive thought of their times, but they were seldom swayed by the fads and the by-ways that often lead liberals in religion to go off on tangents.

William Ware preached a kind of Channing Unitarianism which the people so much wanted to hear, a Biblical interpretation of the reality of the Unity of the Godhead rather than a Trinity of Powers. Henry Bellows carried on Channing's Unitarianism, but he also added his own distinctiveness. Although himself conservative by nature, in his religious thinking, he was constantly seeking to be inclusive, and he was known as a "Broad Church Unitarian" because of his willingness to have a basic agreement on broad principles and to give everyone the right to fill in the details, even if they did not agree with his own.

Theodore Chickering Williams was a poet at heart, and his religion like much of the religious thinking of his contemporaries was clothed in poetics and beautiful words. Thomas Roberts Slicer was a social reformer who worked hard for the reformation of society and inspired others to do the same. He was also a very popular preacher. He believed that Christianity is an individual religion and that unless better individuals were created by a church that society would not get better in spite of new laws and programs.

William Laurence Sullivan was a man of deep spirituality who left the warm bosom of Catholicism to become a Unitarian. He was noted for his religious insights and his ability to move people with his preaching. Minot Simons was a theist and a leader of men and women. His two significant contributions in our history were to move the church to a new location uptown, and to preach a religion that made sense to people. Laurance Irving Neale was a layman who was elected by the congregation to be their minister after he had shown his abilities on the practical side of church management. Not a great preacher, as he started too late in life and never received a theological degree, he preached practical ethics for the person in the pew.

I came to the church at a very difficult time in its history. The congregation has grown very fast under Dr. Neale's leadership, showing that it is not necessarily great preaching that makes a church grow. After the Second World War many families moved into the East Side of New York City, and the church was a family church with a large and well-known Sunday School program.

When I came to All Souls in 1955, I had not realized that a small group had taken over the management of the church and dominated its philosophy. One of the presidents of the board of trustees under whom I served was afraid that there were Communists lurking in the wings of Unitarianism, and he was concerned as a reserve army officer that Unitarians would go off the deep end.

There were also many Jewish immigrants who had come to America to escape Hitler, and they chose a church which had a philosophy with which they agreed. But they wanted very little to do with Judaism after their escape from Hitler. They wanted the church to be distinctly Christian. But there was also a great deal of anti-Semitism among them, and I was never Christian enough for some of them.

My pastorate was the second longest after Henry Bellows. I inherited a church with a large membership, few of whom attended church. That changed rapidly after I came, and often there were few empty seats in the pews. But the mood of the sixties and the seventies became very anti-institutional, and there was a reaction against all churches as simply another of those oppressive institutions. So membership and attendance declined. We were just witnessing a rise in attendance when I retired.

My emphasis was upon a religion that made sense. As a former Presbyterian minister I was wary of professing one thing and really believing another, and I tried to bring history to bear upon religion so that people could link their own religious convictions with those of the past, and built a sensible religion for their own use.

I say not immodestly, that when Forrester Church took over in the fall of 1978, the church was in good condition. It was not necessary to have an interim minister. The invested funds had increased dramatically while I was the minister, and not all of it by far was due to my efforts. Without those funds the church would have found it hard to survive. Attendance was down, but Dr. Church soon took care of that problem with his charisma and ability to get things across to people.

The area around the church had started to change drastically during my ministry for soon families found apartments and private schooling too expensive, and many moved from the city. They were replaced largely by bright young people with good educations and holding prestigious positions in law, finance, business, and the other professions. These people were attracted to Dr. Church's down-to-earth common sense concepts of religion.

Often church histories are too much a history of the ministers, and periods are divided by the terms of the ministries. That is true of All Souls, and it is the more so because the ministries were usually long. But there is a thread of continuity that runs through all of the ministries. It is difficult to say what "The All Souls spirit" is, but I noticed that Dr. Church after a few months found that spirit. He says that he caught it during his first interview with the search committee, and that at that moment he felt "called." It is a spirit that carries on through all of the ministries, and it has been caught by many people in the pews.

Perhaps the spirit of a church is best exemplified not by its ministers or its Sunday services, but how people put their beliefs into action in their private and social lives. When large numbers of immigrants came to New York City in the eighteen-thirties and forties, the various governmental bodies had no plans other than to get them off Ellis Island. They settled down in the various neighborhood ghettos of New York City.

In Volume I. of this history we saw how a ministry to the poor was prompted by the feeling that these people were simply left alone to go their own ways with no social service, no guidance, and much poverty and suffering. The church people rose to the occasion. They set up schools for the immigrant children, they taught the women sewing and various household duties so that they could secure work

During the Civil War as recounted in Volume II., it was the women who responded and set up the United States Sanitary Commission, and, although Henry Bellows served as the president, it was the women who did the work at New York Central at Cooper Union, and who ran the Sanitary Fairs. Just as the Civil War was concluding Henry Bellows was instrumental in calling a conference in New York City to organize the Unitarian denomination, and Bellows and later Thomas Slicer were active in Civil

Service reform. As has been related many of the social service organizations of the city and state were organized by leadership from All Souls Church, everything from nursing schools to social service reform.

In this Volume III., we report how during the First and Second World Wars the women rolled bandages and made warm clothing for the troops overseas. After the Second World war the impact of government had changed, and beginning with the "New Deal" and then "The Great Society" and other social plans, the Federal government began to spend billions of dollars on a wide variety of projects to combat poverty, to increase educational opportunities, and to do many other things of a social improvement nature. The government became the controller of the purse strings, and high taxes were substituted for charities as the great impetus for social change.

In the early days of my ministry All Souls Church was the leader in raising funds for the Unitarian Service Committee. Many lay persons sat on important boards of social organizations. Many believed that this kind of activity was more effective than signing resolutions.

Perhaps this is the best test of how religion is operating in the lives of people: how they treat their fellow humans, and how they roll up their sleeves and help with problems such as suffering, AIDS, poverty, and the like.

There has also been a plethora of talent in the church among the members. This quality perhaps reached its highest point when Dr. Neale was the minister. Late in his ministry he made a survey of the church membership which was then calculated to be about eleven hundred persons, and compared the membership list with *Who's Who in America*. It turned out that there were fifty-three members of the church in *Who's Who*. This may not be a test which is accurate, but it gave some indication as to the quality of the congregation. A study of the history of All Souls shows that the members of the church always took their civic duties seriously, and that they were concerned about building a better city and nation. Several actively entered local politics.

A church with a history as long as that of All Souls of necessity has many traditions which are important in the life of the church. Probably the most important of these is that there has been a strong tradition of lay leadership in the church. In fact, this is one of a very few large churches where a lay person has been chosen to be the minister when the qualities of the ministers available did not seem to be what the church needed in 1941 when Dr. Minot Simons died. Mr. Neale proved to be the right person at the right time.

During all of the years of its history lay participation was strong. This was particularly so during the difficult times when prominent men served year after year as trustees, culminating in George F. Baker's term of 50 consecutive years on the board of trustees. Today this procedure would probably be called "undemocratic," but it worked.

Another tradition has been that the church has never been led by a minister or a layperson who openly espoused the "new thing," or the "latest fad." Sometimes it is conceived that social action is participating in the current march, or shouting the loudest at a rally, and endeavors such as that. This has never been considered to be proper social action by the people of All Souls. Some of the ministers led the way to new concepts of civil service reform (Bellows and Slicer). My successor, Dr. Church, is adept at pointing out the importance of social needs and problems, and then encouraging the lay people to roll up their sleeves and do the dirty work.

Another tradition at All Souls has been stability. The ministers, with the exception of William Sullivan who was called to "a higher duty" by the Layman's League, have been long. William Ware did resign because he questioned his own ability to preach and to lead his congregation, but he served well as a pastor for fifteen of the difficult early years. Henry Bellows served for 43 years, and was probably the most important churchman that the Unitarians have produced in America. Theodore Williams seemingly lost his zest to preach, and his resignation comes the closest to being a disaster as any other event in the history of All Souls.

There have been crises in the history of All Souls even in the best of times, but the custom has been to accept what has been valuable and to look to the future with confidence because of its proud heritage.

As we have seen in this volume, its members have always been generous to All Souls, especially in the most trying of times when the bank was ready to foreclose the mortgage on the church during World War II. But even in those troublous times the people responded not out of plenty but in a truly sacrificial way.

Thanks to the gifts of Mrs. von Bernuth and Miss Foote, who left a trust to the church on the lives of several of their family, a large sum came to the church. From Maude Perry Mills who worked for *The Children's Encyclopedia,* and the large gift from the John Lindsley Fund, and a wise investment policy, endowments were built up over the years to their present status, which is no longer adequate funding from endowments for an institution as large and active as All Souls has now become.

Doctrinally, All Souls has been on the prudent side in the Unitarian tradition, moving ahead cautiously. This means especially that the right of every person to have his or her own convictions and to have them respected by fellow congregants is of prime importance. All Souls is a church which respects the Christian tradition. Christian is not a "dirty word" at the church. And yet the people generally respect every other religious tradition also. All Souls people do not conform to a pattern. You will find all shades of belief and unbelief. The important thing for the minister always to remember is to state convictions, but to remember, as Dr. Church says, that we all see things in a cathedral in the light of the different kinds of light which stream through the windows. When some would try to force a particular belief on All Souls' people they are in for a hard time. These I believe are the solid traditions of the church.

It has been said that a church is a living organism with its own soul and its own style. One of the reasons that I have spent many hours of my life researching and writing these three volumes on our history is to illustrate the fact that All Souls was not born yesterday, and it did not arrive at where it is today without the valiant struggle of many sincere people through hard and difficult times. There has been much service by many unheralded and unsung men and women that has kept this church alive and strong and serving. It is only when we understand its long and important history that we begin to see the importance of All Souls, and what it can do for the future in its position of leadership in the New York and national community.

Notes:

Prologue:

1. For an account of the ministries of William Ware and Charles Follen, c.f. Walter D. Kring: *Liberals Among the Orthodox: Unitarian Beginnings in New York City,1819-1839,* Beacon Press, Boston, 1974.
2. For a complete account of Bellows see Walter D. Kring: *Henry Whitney Bellows,* Skinner House Press, Boston,1979.
3. Walter Donald Kring, Henry Whitney Bellows, pp. 227 ff.
4. All Souls Minute Book No.3., pp. 12-13.
5. All Souls Minute Book No.3., pp. 14-15.
6. All Souls Minute Book No.3., pp. 16-19.

Chapter 1. *"A Poet At Heart"*

1 From a printed sermon "The Conflict of Duties," November 27, 1892, printed in "The Weekly Exchange" by George H. Ellis, Boston,1892.
2. All Souls Minute Book, Volume 3., p. 60.
3. All Souls Minute Book, Volume 3., pp. 70-71.
4. Kring, *Henry Whitney Bellows,* pp. 282-284.
5. All Souls Minute Book, Volume 3., pp. 72-73.
6. All Souls Minute Book, Volume 3., p. 77.
7. All Souls Minute Book, Volume 3., p. 78.
8. George Herbert Palmer, *Theodore Chickering Williams: A Biographical Sketch,* Harvard University Press, 1915, p. 5.
9. *New York Tribune,* 1883. No date on clipping. Probably fall of 1883 when Williams first came to New York City.
10. Henry Wilder Foote II, *American Unitarian Hymn Writers and Hymns,* Cambridge, Mass, 1959 (mimeograph copy in the Harvard Divinity School Library).

11. Ibid.

12. A complete account of the Sewall hymnal is to be found in Kring, *Liberals Among the Orthodox,* pp. 92-102.

13. c.f. *Henry Whitney Bellows,* p. 474.

14. c.f. *Henry Whitney Bellows,* Appendix B. "Criteria for Church Membership," pp. 479-481.

15. All Souls Minute Book, Vol. 3., p. 342.

16. All Souls Minute Book, Vol. 3., p. 343.

17. All Souls Minute Book, Vol. 3., p. 344.

18. All Souls Minute Book, Vol. 3., p. 346.

9. All Souls Minute Book, Vol. 3., p. 347.

20. All Souls Minute Book, Vol. 3., p. 349.

21. Letters of George R. Bishop written in 1927 in the All Souls archives. Letters is in a poorly written hand, and parts of it have faded. But enough is discernable to indicate that this is an important document in understanding the final year or two of Mr. Williams All Souls pastorate.

22. Samuel A Eliot. *Heralds of A Liberal Faith: The Pilots,* The Beacon Press, Boston, 1952, pp. 254-255.

23. Ibid. p. 235.

24. Ibid. p. 256.

25. George Herbert Palmer, *Theodore Chickering Williams, A Biographical Sketch,* Harvard University Press, 1915, p. 6.

26. Ibid. p. 8.

Chapter 2. "One World at a Time"

1. From the "Foreword" of One World At A Time, by Thomas Roberts Slicer, G. P Putnam's Sons, New York, 1902, p. VII.

2. All Souls Minute Book, Vol. 3., p. 359.

3. Letter by George R. Bishop in the All Souls archives.

4. Ibid.

5. All Souls Minute Book, Vol. 3., p. 379.

6. All Souls Minute Book, Vol. 3., p. 385.

7. Ibid.

8. The complete letter can be found in All Souls Minute Book, Vol. 3., pp. 385-386.

9. All Souls Minute Book, Vol. 3., p. 398.

10. All Souls Minute Book, Vol. 3., p. 401.

11. *Dictionary of American Biography.*

12. All Souls Minute Book, Vol. 3., p. 410.

13. Ibid.

14. William Bennett Munro in *Dictionary of American Biography.*

15. Letter of George R. Bishop in All Souls archives, dated December 14, 1927.

16. Samuel A. Eliot, *Heralds of a Liberal Faith,* Vol 3, The American Unitarian Association, Boston, 1952, pp. 257-257.

17. "Memorial" to Horace J. Hayden in All Souls Minute Book, Vol. 3., pp. 454-455.

18. All Souls Minute Book, Vol. 3., pp. 429-430.

19. Manuscript in the All Souls archives, pp. 4, 4A.

20. Ibid. p. 6A, 7.

21. Ibid. p. 7A.

22. Ibid. pp. 8A, 9.

23. Ibid. pp. 13, 13A.

24. All Souls Minute Book, Vol. 3, pp. 478-479.

25. Quoted in a letter from George R. Bishop in the All Souls archives, December 14, 1927.

26. Ibid.

27. Letter in the All Souls archives

Chapter 3. "A Spirit Aflame"

1. *New York Tribune,* May 31, 1919.

2. Max Dascom, The Flaming Spirit, Abingdon Press, New York, 1961, p. 13. Mr. Dascom tells this story as well as the one about the tonsure ceremony, p. 20.

3. Minot Simons "Address at the Unveiling of a Memorial Tablet to William Laurence Sullivan, March 26, 1939." All

Souls archives.

4. Ibid.

5. File of "Faith and Freedom" in the All Souls Archives.

6. "Faith and Freedom," Vol. 1., No. 1., p. 2.

7. Ibid. p. 3.

8. Handwritten note in All Souls Archives, dated January 15, 1917.

9. "Faith and Freedom," Vol. 1. No. 5, p. 1.

10. All Souls Minute Book, Volume 4, pp. 138-139.

11. John Haynes Holmes, *I Speak for Myself,* Harper & Brothers, New York, 1959, p. 92.

12. Ibid., p. 87.

13. Ibid., p. 88.

14. All Souls Minute Book, Vol. 4., p. 177.

15. Ibid.

16. Ibid., p. 178.

17. Ibid.

18. Ibid., p. 201.

19. Ibid.

20. All Souls Minute Book, Volume 4., p. 260.

21. Ibid.

22. Ibid, p. 272.

23. Ibid.

24. Ibid.

25. cf. Kring, *Henry Whitney Bellows,* pp. 479-481.

26. This is the covenant of the Unitarian Church of All Souls of New York City today except that the last phrase has been changed to read from "the service of man" to "the service of all."

27. All Souls Minute Book, Volume 4. pp. 275-276.

28. I had some personal talks with William Nichols, one of the trustees who resigned. He was the president of the board of trustees for several years during my ministry, and he told me that Dr. Sullivan's plan for a group ministry was simply not acceptable.

29. John Ratte: *Three Modernists: Alfred Loisy, George Tyrrell, William L. Sullivan,* Sheed and Ward, London, 1968.

30. Ibid. p. 275.

31. Ibid. p. 276.
32. Ibid. P. 277.
33. Ibid. p. 283.
34. Ibid. p. 287.
35. Ibid. p. 289.
36. *Letter to His Holiness Pope Pius X,* William L. Sullivan, Chicago, 1910, p. xviii.
37. Ibid. p. 166.
38. "William Laurence Sullivan: An Appreciation," T*he Christian Register,* November 16, 1935.
39. Samuel A. Eliot, Heralds of *A Liberal Faith; The Pilots,* Volume IV, Beacon Press, Boston, 1952, p. 238.
40. Quoted in the leaflet at the Unveiling of the Sullivan Memorial Tablet, in the All Souls archives.
41. Ibid.
42. Ratte, *Three Modernists,* p. 328.
43. Minot Simons, "Address at the Unveiling of a Memorial Tablet to William Laurence Sullivan, D.O.." March 26, 1939, All Souls archives.

Chapter 4. *"A Builder Arrives"*

1. Minot Simons, *A Modern Theism,* The Beacon Press, Boston, 1931, pp. 61-62.
2. All Souls Minute Book, Volume 4., p. 287.
3. Church Calendar, May 8,1923.
4. Ibid.
5. Church Calendar, April 29,1923.
6. Church Calendar for June 9,1929.
7. From the manuscript in the All Souls archives.
8. All Souls archives
9. All Souls Minute Book, Volume 4, pp. 54-55.
10. Kring, *Liberals Among the Orthodox,* pp. 22-24.
11. Church Calendar for March 14,1940.
12. Ibid.

13. Church Calendar for December 8, 1940.

14. "Minot Simons" by Laurance I. Neale, a memorial sermon delivered at the Church of All Souls in New York City," June 8, 1941.

Chapter 5. "A Preacher from the Pews."

1. From a printed sermon "Powerhouse of the Spirit" delivered on September 19, 1943. All Souls archives.

2. All Souls Minute Book, Volume 5., p. 438.

3. Letter from Minot Simons to Frederick May Eliot, May 12, 1941, U.U.A. archives.

4. Memorial Service for Minot Simons and Albert Williams, May 24, 1942, Memorial Booklet, pp. 17-18., All Souls archives.

5. All Souls Minute Book, Volume 5., p. 473.

6. All Souls Minute Book, Volume 6., p. 1.

7. Ibid.

8. Ibid.

9. Ibid.

10. All Souls Minute Book, Volume 5., p. 6.

11. All Souls Minute Book, Volume 6., p. 16.

12. Ibid., p. 168.

13. Ibid., p. 187.

14. Ibid.

15. All of this material is in a manuscript report of the Victory Dinner, All Souls archives.

16. Act of Consecration, 125th Anniversary Service, All Souls archives.

17. Ibid.

18. The complete list of the members of families connected with All Souls who were in the armed forces is to be found in the Church Calendar for November 12,1944.

19. All Souls Minute Book, Volume 6, pp. 274-275.

20. Ibid., p. 293.

21. Ibid., p. 441

22. Biography of Charles Howard Strong in the All Souls archives.
23. *Dictionary of American Biography,* The article was written by Ernest Sutherland Bates.
24. Printed program, All Souls archives.
25. All Souls Minute Book, Volume 7., p. 251.
26. 1955 Annual Report, Ibid. p. 321. Also copies in the Church archives.
27. Ibid.
28. Church Calendar for June 19, 1955.
29. Church Calendar for April 8,1956.

Chapter 6. *"A Potter Shapes the Church"*

1. From Walter Donald Kring, *Religion Is the Search for Meaning,* The Starr King Press, Boston, 1955. p. 5.
2. Minute Book, Volume 7, p. 350.
3. Minute Book, Volume 7, p. 356
4. Minute Book, Volume 7., p. 358.
5. Church Calendar for September 19,1955.
6. For a genealogy of the Kring Family, see Horner & Bickell, *From Sea to Shining Sea: The Kring Family;* Privately Printed,1980.
7. Anyone who is interested in Kring's ministry in Worcester should consult: Kring: *The Fruits of Our Labors: The Bicentennial History of the Second Parish in the Town of Worcester, First Unitarian Church; 1785-1985*, Published by the First Unitarian Church of Worcester, 1985, pp. 173-190.
8. See The Installation Program, Church Archives, for a list of the Guests of Honor.
9. Church Calendar for December 26, 1971.
10. See Church Calendar for December 4,1977.
11. Church Calendar for September 21, 1958. A more detailed study of the scroll is to be found in "The Riddle of the All Souls Deuteronomy" by Walter Donald Kring in *The Unitarian Universalist Christian,* Summer 1972, Volume 27, no. 2. pp. 32-42.

12. Church Calendar for September 14, 1958.

13. Annual Report for 1960, p. 5.

14. Church Calendar for June 5,1966.

15. c.f. Kring: Henry Whitney Bellows, pp. 189-204.

16. Church Calendar for September 11, 1966.

17. c.f. Walter D. Kring and Jonathan Carey: "Two Discoveries Concerning Herman Melville," Proceedings of the Massachusetts Historical Society, 87 (1975) pp. 137-141. Or c.f. Walter D. Kring: Henry Whitney Bellows, Skinner House, Unitarian Universalist Association, Boston, 1979, pp. 344-346.

18. See The Christian Register for March, 1959, p. 7.

19. Church Calendar for September 21, 1969.

20. Church Calendar for September 27, 1970.

21. Church Calendar for June 7,1964.

22. Annual Report for 1964.

23. Church Calendar for December 29, 1968.

24. Report of the Annual Meeting of 1957, p. 7.

25. Church Calendar for January 19, 1969.

26. Church Calendar for May 31, 1964.

27. See Church Calendar for October 2, 1977 for a letter by Mrs. Ganley about why the Ganley's joined All Souls Church.

28. Copy in Church Archives.

Chapter 7. "Realizing a Great Vision"

1. From F. Forrester Church, *Father and Son,* Faber and Faber, Boston, 1985, pp. 178-179.

2. F. Forrester Church, "How My Mind Has Changed," September 25, 1988. Sermon preached at All Souls Church.

3. Ibid.

3. Ibid.

4. Ibid.

5. Ibid.

APPENDIX A

Officers of the Unitarian Church of All Souls 1881-1978

Trustees nominally were elected for a three-year term. Sometimes in case of death, resignation, or removal from the city, they were not immediately replaced. The president or chairman was usually elected at the first meeting of the trustees by the trustees, but in practice the same person also became the president of the congregation. Under each year only those elected that year are listed. After each name is the number of years served.

1882 President: J. Harson Rhoades (1880-1896)
Trustees:
Nathan Chandler (15)
Emerson Foote (13)
J. Harsen Rhoades (33)
William T. Wardwell (12)

1883 Minister: Theodore Chickering Williams (1883-1896)
Trustees:
Benjamin S. Arnold (28)
Samuel B. Dana (10) James M. Drake (2)

1884 Trustees:
George F. Baker (50)
Addison Brown (19)
William M. Prichard (41)
Sidney S. Smith (14)

William T. Wardwell (12)

1892 Trustees:
George R. Bishop (39)
Theodore B. Starr (2)

1893 Trustees:
George F. Baker (50)
Daniel A. Davis (22)
Richard H. Ewart (14)
Sidney S. Smith (14)

1894 Trustees:
Benjamin S. Arnold (28)
Horace J. Hayden (11)
J. Harsen Rhoades (33)

1895 Trustees:
George R. Bishop (39)
J. Lawrence McKeever (21)

1896 President: J. Lawrence McKeever 1896-1897
Trustees:
George F. Baker (50)
Richard H. Ewart (14)
Daniel A. Davis (22)

1897 Minister: Thomas Roberts Slicer (1897-1916)
Trustees:
Frederick P. Forster (15)
Horace J. Hayden (11)
J. Harsen Rhoades (33)

1898 Trustees:
George R. Bishop (39)
J. Lawrence McKeever (21)

1899 Trustees:
George F. Baker (50)
Daniel A. Davis (22)
Richard H. Ewart (14)
Franklin A. Wilcox (9)

1900 President: Horace J. Hayden, 1900-1902
Trustees:
Frederick P. Forster (15)
J. Harsen Rhoades (33)
Horace J. Hayden (11)

1901 Trustees:
George R. Bishop (39)
J. Lawrence McKeever (21)
Charles H. Strong (20)

1902 President: J. Lawrence, McKeever, 1902-1913
Trustees:
George F. Baker 50)
Daniel A. Davis (22)
Franklin A. Wilcox (9)

1903 Trustees:
Frederick P. Forster (15)
J. Harsen Rhoades (33)

1904 Trustees:
George R. Bishop (39)
J. Lawrence McKeever (21)
Charles H. Strong (20)

1905 Trustees:
George F. Baker (50)
Daniel A. Davis (22)
Franklin A. Wilcox (9)

1906 Trustees:
Frederick P. Forster (15)
Philip W. Harding (3)

1907 Trustees:
George R. Bishop (39)
J. Lawrence McKeever (21)
Charles H. Strong (20)

1908 Trustees:
George F. Baker (50)
Daniel A. Davis (22)

1909 Trustees:
Frederick P. Forster (15)
Alexander J. Hemphill (11)

1910 Trustees:
George R. Bishop (39)
J. Lawrence McKeever (21)
Lucius H. Nutting (14)
Charles H. Strong (20)

1911 Trustees:
George F. Baker (50)
Daniel A. Davis (22)

1912 Trustees:
Alexander J. Hemphill (11)

1913 President: Daniel A. Davis 1913-1915
Trustees:
George R. Bishop (39)
Alexander V. Fraser (7)
J. Lawrence McKeever (21)

Lucius H. Nutting (14) Charles H. Strong (20)

1914 Trustees:
George F. Baker (50)
Daniel A. Davis (22)

1915 President: Alexander J. Hemphill 1915-1919
Trustees: Alexander J. Hemphill (11)

1916 Minister: William Laurence Sullivan (1916-1932)
Trustees:
George R. Bishop (39)
Warren Delano (4)
Alexander V. Fraser (7)
E. Morgan Grinnell (9)
Lucius H. Nutting (14)
Charles H. Strong (20)

1917 Trustees:
George F. Baker (50)

1918 Trustees:
Alexander J. Hemphill (11)

1919 President: Charles H. Strong 1919-1921
Trustees:
George R. Bishop (39)
Warren Delano (4)
Alexander V. Fraser (7)
E. Morgan Grinnell (11)
R. H. Kissel (3)
Lucius H. Nutting (14)
Charles H. Strong (20)

1920 Trustees:
George F. Baker (50)

Charles P. Blaney (9)

1921 President: R. H. Kissel 1921- 1923
Trustees:
Dr. William B. Dunning (3)
Robert Ramsey (2)

1922 Trustees:
Richard Billings (4)
George R. Bishop (39)
John W. Draper (3)
E. Morgan Grinnell (11)
Rudolph C. Neuendorffer (21)
William B. Nichols (6)
Lucius H. Nutting (14)

1923 President: Richard Billings 1923
Trustees:
George F. Baker (50)
Charles P. Blaney (9)
Mrs. John R. McGinley (6)
Laurance I. Neale (14)
Georgina Schuyler (2)

1924 President: Laurance I Neale (1923-192=6)
Trustees:
Mrs. Malcolm Goodridge (3)
Mrs. William Herbert (3)
Francis Rogers (9)

1925 Trustees:
George R. Bishop (39)
Rudolph C. Neuendorffer (21)

1926 Trustees;
George F. Baker (50)

Charles P. Blaney (9)
Mrs. John R. McGinley (6)
Laurance I. Neale (14)

1927 President: Rudolph Neuendorffer (1927-1936)
Trustees:
Francis Rogers (9)

1928 Trustees:
Elliot Stuart Benedict (10)
George R. Bishop (39)
Wyman D. Herbert (6)
Rudolph C. Neuendorffer (21)

1929 Trustees:
George F. Baker (50)
Laurance I. Neale (14)
William B. Nichols (6)

1930 Trustees:
Richard Billings (4)
Francis Rogers (9)

1931 Trustees:
George Baker (2nd) (2)
Elliot Stuart Benedict (10)
Lawrence I. Grinnell (3)
Wyman D. Herbert (6)
Mark W. Maclay (21)
Rudolph C. Neuendorffer (21)

1932 Trustees:
Dr. William B. Dunning (3)
Laurance I. Neale (14)
Mrs. Warren Pond (2)
Mrs. William L. Voigt (3)

1933 Minister: Minot Osgood Simons (1923-1941)
Trustees:
Mrs. Walter C. Booth (3)
Gilman S. Stanton (3)
Albert H. Wiggin (3)

1934 Trustees:
Elliot Stuart Benedict (10)
John W. Corney (3)
Parker Morse Hooper (2)
Mark W. Maclay (21)
Rudolph C. Neuendorffer (21)

1935 Trustees:
Dr. N. Chandler Foot (5)
Dr. Redford K. Johnson (4)
Henry C. Lamb (1)
Mrs. Anita Pearson (3)

1936 Trustees:
Mrs. William B. Dunning (3)
Frederick W. Ecker (3)

1937 President: Laurance I. Neale (1937-1939)
Trustees:
Elliot Stuart Benedict (10)
Mark W. Maclay (21)
Laurance I. Neale (14)
Rudolph C. Neuendorffer (21)

1938 Trustees:
Dr. Alfred Ehrenclou (3)
Dr. N. Chandler Foot (5)
Mrs. Leonard Poore (2)

1939 Trustees:
Mrs. Theodore Hope (3)
Frederick Augustus von Bernuth, Jr. (3)

1940 President: Mark W. Maclay 1940-1948
Trustees:
Elliot Stuart Benedict (10)
Ralph Gaqscoigne Brown (3)
Dr. William B. Dunning (8)
Mark W. Maclay (21)
Newton Monk (2)
Laurance I. Neale (14)

1941 Trustees:
Dr. RobertS. Grinnelll (6)

1942 Minister: Laurance Irving Neale (1942-1955)
Trustees:
Mrs. Elizabeth Draper (3)
George Adams Ellis (3)

1943 Trustees:
Elliot Stuart Benedict (10)
William Arthur Berridge (3)
Mark W. Maclay (21)

1944 Trustees:
Dr. Alfred Ehrenclou (3)
Otto Frederick Langmann (3)
Miss Margaret Roys (3)

1945 Trustees:
Mrs. Irma Miller Amberg (3)
Francis Abbot Goodhue (3)

Joseph Frederick Sharp (2)

1953 Trustees:
Charles Oliver Wellington (3)
Louise Lawrence White (3)
Donald B. Woodward (3)

1954 Trustees:
Mrs. Cora M. Ehrenclou (3)
Rolf Kaltenborn 2)
Samuel B. Payne (3)

1955 Minister: Walter Donald Kring (1955-1978)
President: Raymond S. Fanning 1955-1958
Trustees:
Alvin Devereux (3)
Raymond S. Fanning (6)
Charles Chester Lane (10)
Marion Read Maclay (3)

1956 Trustees:
Mrs. Virginia Collins
Duncombe (2)
Samuel Morse Lane (10)
Herman Seid (5)
John Eliot Woodbridge (3)

1957 Trustees:
Mrs. Marjorie M. Raeburn (6)
Robert Rinear (3)
Dr. Nelson B. Sackett (6)
Mrs. Mary D. Wappler (6)

1958 Trustees:
Philip Lukin (3)
Miss Florence McKinlay (7)

1959 President: Samuel M. Lane
Trustees:
Frederick L. Strong (6)
Samuel Morse Lane (10)
William C. Wallstein (6)

1960 President: Charles Chester Lane, 1960
Trustees:
William B. Nichols (6)
Charles M. Sherover (3)
Mrs. Mary Danforth Wappler (6)

1961 President: Miss Florence McKinlay, 1961-1962
Trustees:
Miss Martha Allen (3)
E. Eugene Grossman (6)
Miss Florence McKinlay (4)
Herman Seid (6)

1962 President: William B. Nichols
Trustees:
Arsene Charles Bekaert (3)
Lawrence Royce Chenault (5)
Alfred M. Ehrenclou (3)

1963 President: E. Eugene Grossman, 1963-1967
Trustees:
Arne Howell Groningsater (3)
Greene F. Johnson (3)
Miss Margaret Smith (3)

1964 Trustees:
E. Eugene Grossman (6)
Murray Leigh (3)
Mrs. Harry Russell (3)

1965 Trustees:
Shuyler G. Chapin (6)
Lawrence Royce Chenault (5)
Eleanor Clark French (6)
Phyllis C. Hadley (3)

1966 Trustees:
Samuel Morse Lane (10)
William C. Wallstein (6)

1967 President: William C. Wallstein 1967
Trustees:
Reynold Bennett (2)
Edward N. Costikyan (5)
Alvin Devereux (6)
Francisca Ehrenclou (3)
Dr. Maurice Green (2)

1968 President: Edward N. Costikyan, 1968-1969
Trustees:
Walter Hindle (3)
Robert Reagan (3)

1969 Trustees:
Stephen Dietz (5)
James French (3)
Mrs. Jeanne Walton (3)

1970 President: W. Stephens Dietz (1970-1974)
Trustees:
Edward N. Costikyan (5)
Mrs. Murray S. Leigh (3)
Oscar M. Miller (6)

1971 Trustees:
Sandra Mitchell Caron (6)

Patricia Morrill (3)

1978 President: Maxine Beshers
Trustees:
Elizabeth Delman (3)
Joseph Hellman (3)
Bert Zippel (3)

Index

St. Gaudens, Augustus: 13, 89, 90
Santa Ana Junior College: 149
Savage, Helen L.: 83
Savage, Maxwell: 58, 83, 153
Savage, Minot J.: 20, 27, 58, 59, 83
Savior, Church of the: vi, 173
Schuyler, Georgina: 70, 81, 85
Schuyler, Louisa L.: 85
Scovel, Carl R.: 173, 174
Scriabin, Alexander: 158
Second Church in Boston: 209
Sewall Hymnbook: 13
Shaaray Tefila: 164
Sherry, Henry A.: 90
Sherover, Charles: 198
Sichel, Mrs. Harold: 84
Simons, Minot 0.: 27, 51, 66, 70, 75 - 84, 95, 105, 109, 110
Slap, Charles: 173, 174, 180
Slicer, Thomas R.: 20, 27, 28, 30-39, 41, 42, 45, 46, 52, 101, 220, 222, 224,
Smith, Sally: 210
Smith, Sidney: 18, 29, 35
Soares, Theodore: 80
Society for Relief & Employment of Poor Women: 175
South Boston Navy Yard: 153
Spence Chapin Adoption: 205, 210
Sperry, Dean Willard: 150
Spofford, Miss Grace: 181
Stansfield, Otto: 91
State Charities Aid Assn: 85
Stebbins, Roderick: 24
Stefansson, Vilhajalmur: 110
Steiner, Richard: 146
Stendahl, Krister: 170, 218
Stewart, Mrs. Richard: 32

Made in the USA
Middletown, DE
07 April 2019